ETHICS FOR ENEMIES

UEHIRO SERIES IN PRACTICAL ETHICS

General Editor: Julian Savulescu, University of Oxford

Choosing Children
The Ethical Dilemmas of Genetic Intervention
Jonathan Glover

Messy Morality
The Challenge of Politics
C. A. J. Coady

Killing in War
Jeff McMahan

Beyond Humanity?
The Ethics of Biomedical Enhancement
Allen Buchanan

Ethics for Enemies
Terror, Torture, and War
F. M. Kamm

ETHICS FOR ENEMIES
TERROR, TORTURE, AND WAR

F. M. KAMM

OXFORD
UNIVERSITY PRESS

OXFORD
UNIVERSITY PRESS

Great Clarendon Street, Oxford OX2 6DP

Oxford University Press is a department of the University of Oxford.
It furthers the University's objective of excellence in research, scholarship,
and education by publishing worldwide in

Oxford New York

Auckland Cape Town Dar es Salaam Hong Kong Karachi
Kuala Lumpur Madrid Melbourne Mexico City Nairobi
New Delhi Shanghai Taipei Toronto

With offices in

Argentina Austria Brazil Chile Czech Republic France Greece
Guatemala Hungary Italy Japan Poland Portugal Singapore
South Korea Switzerland Thailand Turkey Ukraine Vietnam

Oxford is a registered trade mark of Oxford University Press
in the UK and in certain other countries

Published in the United States
by Oxford University Press Inc., New York

British Library Cataloguing in Publication Data

Data available

Library of Congress Cataloging in Publication Data

Data available

Typeset by SPI Publisher Services, Pondicherry, India
Printed in Great Britain
on acid-free paper by
MPG Books Group, Bodmin and King's Lynn

ISBN 978–0–19–960878–2

1 3 5 7 9 10 8 6 4 2

The Uehiro Series in Practical Ethics

In 2002 the Uehiro Foundation on Ethics and Education, chaired by Mr Eiji Uehiro, established the Uehiro Chair in Practical Ethics at the University of Oxford. The following year the Oxford Uehiro Centre for Practical Ethics was created within the Philosophy Faculty. Generous support by the Uehiro Foundation enabled the establishment of an annual lecture series, The Uehiro Lectures in Practical Ethics. These three lectures, given each year in Oxford, capture the ethos of the Oxford Uehiro Centre for Practical Ethics: to bring the best scholarship in analytic philosophy to bear on the most significant problems of our time. The aim is to make progress in the analysis and resolution of these issues to the highest academic standard in a manner that is accessible to the general public. Philosophy should not only create knowledge, it should make people's lives better. Books based upon the lectures are published by Oxford University Press in the Uehiro Series in Practical Ethics.

Julian Savulescu
Uehiro Chair in Practical Ethics
Director, Oxford Uehiro Centre for Practical Ethics, University of Oxford
Editor, The Uehiro Series in Practical Ethics

In memory of my uncle,
Samuel Kamm,
with thanks for his crucial help at crucial times

CONTENTS

INTRODUCTION

This book is composed of revised versions of the three Uehiro Lectures that I gave at Oxford University in November–December 2008. I am very grateful to Professor Julian Savulescu, head of the Uehiro Centre for Practical Ethics at Oxford University, for having invited me to give these lectures.

For the most part, the book considers how certain distinctions that I have explored in my work on ethical theory bear on aspects of the practical problems of terrorism, torture, and war.[1] (I emphasize "aspects," as I do not attempt to provide a complete discussion of these problems.) In general, after working on certain issues in ethical theory, I often become aware of how these same issues arise in practical contexts. This is how, in the past, I came to write on several topics in bioethics, such as allocation of scarce resources and physician-assisted suicide. My interest in terrorism, torture, and war arose in the same way. By contrast, others may begin with a deep concern about the practical problems themselves. However, considering the practical problems, I find, can also help uncover new considerations and distinctions and so lead to revisions in one's ethical theory.

My method in dealing with both ethical theory and practical issues makes heavy use of hypothetical cases. Such cases can be varied at will. One can thus test whether a factor is morally significant by comparing the moral status of a case with the factor and a case without the factor, holding all other factors in the cases constant. While the cases may sometimes seem unrealistic, they are somewhat like artificial, controlled experiments in science that eventually yield results for real-life situations.

Chapter 1, "Torture: During and After Action," considers whether those who are responsible for creating lethal threats may be tortured during and after their threatening acts to stop those acts or harm from them. I consider different conceptions of torture and the different occasions when torture might occur in order to isolate factors relevant to the moral status of torturing a wrongdoer held captive. I have previously written on the inviolability of nonthreatening persons. This chapter considers *what* may and may not be done to threatening persons and *when*.

Chapter 2, "Terrorism and Intending Evil," is primarily concerned with whether intending to harm a civilian can account for the special wrongness of terrorism, and also whether such an intention is always an indication of the presence of terrorism. This chapter deals with a practical application of the theoretical question, whether the intention with which an act is done bears on the act's permissibility.

Chapter 3, "Reasons for Starting War: Goals, Conditions, and Proportionality," is also, in part, concerned with whether having a proper intention is necessary in order to make action permissible, in this case, starting war. It goes on to consider how the theoretical distinction between acting in order to bring about a good effect and acting on condition that one will bring it about may bear on the permissibility of causing side-effect harm (sometimes called collateral damage) to civilians in war. The aim is to determine whether and how bad side effects can be proportional to the good effects of war so that we may pursue a just cause by means of war.

A recurring theme of these chapters is whether prohibitions that have been thought to be based on considerations that make an act wrong in itself may rather be based on consequentialist considerations, if they are prohibitions at all. That is, we ask whether certain prohibitions are justified on the ground that what they rule out is intrinsically wrong or rather on the ground that the consequences of acting in certain ways, and features of agents who would act, might rule out certain conduct.

The chapters are self-contained and each may be read on its own. Each has its own conclusion and acknowledgments. However, I am especially grateful to those who have read all three chapters and also provided challenging philosophical discussion, including Ruth Chang, Johann Frick, Shelly Kagan, Jeff McMahan, Derek Parfit, Julian Savulescu, and Larry Temkin. Lynne Meyer Gay's skills were crucial to preparing the manuscript. I am most indebted to Derek Parfit and Thomas Scanlon for their intelligence, kindness, and support over the years.

Note

1. For the theoretical discussion, see, for example, my *Intricate Ethics: Rights, Responsibilities, and Permissible Harm* (New York: Oxford University Press, 2007).

TORTURE: DURING AND AFTER ACTION

Nowadays when we hear the word torture, we think of wrongful, brutal treatment of people in custody whose use in the "war on terror" has recently been a matter of great concern. But sometimes we seem to be tempted to apply the word torture to cases that are unlike this. We may wonder whether doing this is correct and begin to think about the characteristics in virtue of which we identify something as torture. We may also wonder what specific characteristics of wrongful torture make it wrong. Is it just the fact that it is torture? Or is it possible that we need not be misidentifying behavior as torture if we think that the behavior is morally permissible? This chapter is about these issues.

In *Intricate Ethics*,[1] I wrote concerning universal human rights:

There are at least two ways in which the claim that there are such human rights can be understood: (1) All that is needed in order to come to have certain rights is that one be a human person. (2) All that is needed in order to *come to have and continue to have* certain rights is that one be a human person. While there may be some rights that satisfy (2), most rights that are now considered human rights do not satisfy it. They only satisfy (1). For example, the right to free movement, the right not to be killed, and the right to free speech may all be forfeited in virtue of one's conduct. Hence, if there are human rights in sense (1), this does not mean that every human person always has such rights just in virtue of being a human person.

Consider some practical implications of this. Some argue against capital punishment on the ground that it violates a human right not to be killed. They favor incarceration instead. But in the same sense (1) in which there is a right not to be killed, there is a right not to be deprived of liberty. If one can forfeit a right to liberty by bad acts and so can be permissibly incarcerated as punishment, then it is not clear why one could not forfeit the right not to be killed (even when one is not presently a threat). Some argue that there is a human right not to be tortured. Others argue that it would take the need to stop a ticking bomb that threatens an enormous number of people to justify torturing even those who set the bomb. But suppose that a villain is about to set a bomb that will shortly kill one child. Presumably, the villain has no right that we not kill him, if only this would stop his setting the bomb. Furthermore, torturing someone for a short period seems less bad for him than death. Then why does the villain also have no right not to be tortured, if torturing him rather than killing him would also stop his setting the bomb? And if we are unable to kill him, but only able to torture him in order to stop his setting the bomb, might he not also have no right not to be tortured?

This chapter reconsiders some issues in that short discussion by examining aspects of two prominent discussions of torture by Henry Shue[2] and David Sussman.[3] Their discussions raise conceptual issues—that is, what torture is—that might help us decide whether we could correctly apply the term to doing what stops the villain from killing the child. Their discussions also raise normative issues—that is, whether there is something morally distinctive about torture and whether torture is impermissible on deontological rather than on consequentialist grounds. (That is, whether torture is wrong just in virtue of what we would do, independent of whether it would have further bad effects.) I shall critically examine Shue's and Sussman's discussions and try to present an alternative perspective.

In this discussion, I shall focus primarily on cases in which (what might be) torture would be used on people (a) when evidence arrived at independently of torture conclusively shows them to be wrongdoers (e.g., terrorists) and (b) when their being tortured is the only way to get something we need (c) to certainly stop the imminent success of their own murderous plot.[4] This excludes cases where torture is most likely to be morally wrong because (i) it is done to people not known to be wrongdoers in order to find evidence that they are wrongdoers, (ii) it is done to those whom one knows are innocent as a means of stopping someone else's murderous plots, (iii) it is done to acquire what is not necessary to stop a threat or may have only a small chance of stopping a threat, and (iv) it is done when there is no certain and imminent murderous threat to stop.

There has been much philosophical discussion of why it would be wrong to deliberately kill one innocent person to stop other innocent people from being killed by a wrongdoer. My own preferred explanation of this is in terms of the moral status of every innocent person, which rules out the *permissibility* of violating them seriously.[5] I shall assume that the status of such persons would also prevent us from torturing them to save other innocents from being murdered. The question is whether this status is retained by a wrongdoer responsible for the imminent murderous plot against those innocents.

As I have said, the topic of torture has been raised for many by the treatment of prisoners by the United States and some of its allies following the September 11, 2001 attack on the World Trade Center in New York City and the war in Afghanistan. My discussion does not attempt to deal with these actions in particular, as this would require detailed empirical information. However, it does bear on how these actions should be evaluated, given full knowledge of what they involved, and it bears on strategies some have used to deny that these actions involved torture. It is important to remember that even if a discussion of torture showed that it could be morally permissible in some cases, this need not imply that any torture that might have been carried out by the United States or its allies was permissible.[6]

I. *Conceptual Issues*

First, let us consider the conceptual issues with only minimal attention to moral issues they raise. That is, let us consider what torture is, by contrast to other types of behavior, with only minimal attention to whether it (or they) are permissible.

A. SHUE

Shue emphasizes that his characterization of torture is based on torture as it is commonly practiced (at the time he wrote). He is not claiming to offer a conceptual analysis and he concedes that there are many types of hypothetical cases besides the cases he considers that could involve torture.[7] I think it will be useful to consider why cases of torture need not be limited to those Shue considers.

Shue characterizes torture as the infliction of severe distress on someone at a time when he presents no threat and is defenseless. (In the cases he discusses, the person also does not consent to the distress and it is not in his overall interest.) It is these facts, he thinks, that make torture morally problematic. He says that even if being tortured were less bad for someone than being killed, the fact that we may permissibly kill combatants does not show that we may permissibly torture someone we hold in custody. The primary reason for this moral conclusion, he thinks, is that just war theory distinguishes between the permissibility of deliberately killing combatants and the impermissibility of deliberately harming noncombatants[8] based on the inability of the latter to defend themselves against attack (i.e., their being defenseless) (p. 128), and the person who would be tortured is also defenseless against his torturers. Shue thinks that concern for "a fair fight" (p. 130) underlies the combatant/noncombatant moral distinction and it implies that torture victims should be grouped with noncombatants.

My first concern about Shue's view is that his account of the distinction between combatants and noncombatants that is supposed to account for a moral difference between them is not correct. It is commonly thought that the fact that combatants, but not noncombatants, present a threat (at least an unjust one) makes deliberate harm permissible only to the former. Individuals who have set off a missile against us *could be defenseless* against our counterattack because their new missiles are slow to arrive. Yet just war theory does not imply that these individual are not combatants. Nor does it imply that it is impermissible for us to counterattack to stop their further threat on the grounds that there is no "fair fight" until their missiles arrive. Or individual A could be wrongfully attacking innocent B, and while not defenseless against B's counterattacks, A could be defenseless against third party C's attacks when C comes to the aid of B. Presumably this does not mean that A could not be a combatant or make it impermissible for C to stop A's attack on B. Indeed, the more defenseless A is relative to C's attacks on him, the better.

On the other hand, individuals who present no threat could have defenses against an attack on them; though they threaten no one, they have a shield with which to interfere with the attack on them. Presumably, their *not* being defenseless does not mean they are not noncombatants nor does it make it permissible to attack them in the way combatants are attacked.

Hence, even if someone who will be tortured is defenseless, this is neither sufficient nor necessary to distinguish his status (moral or otherwise) from a combatant's.

Eventually, Shue does raise the issue of not being a threat (even if he does not clearly distinguish it from being defenseless). For example, he says, "In combat the other person one kills is still a threat when killed.... The torturer inflicts pain and damage upon another person who...is no longer a threat and is entirely at the torturer's mercy" (p. 130). (See also p. 129.) Insofar as the tortured person is not a threat, he is like the noncombatant as ordinarily understood. But even if it were true of commonly practiced torture that its victims both are not threats and have no defenses, this need not be true of all cases of torture (as Shue might concede). Consider the following case: Someone presents no threat and is given a shield as a physical means of defense against a guard who is trying to cause him continuous severe distress in order to get him to give information. This defense, which could have been successful, fails and the guard succeeds in causing him severe distress. Intuitively, I think it would be wrong to say that this is not a case of torture simply because the victim has a possible physical means of defense.

This leads to the next possibility: Why should the use of the term "torture" be limited to cases where the tortured person does not now present a threat to anyone? For consider the following Killer Case (1), which is like one of the cases I considered in the quote above from *Intricate Ethics*: Person A is trying to kill innocent, nonthreatening person B. A is morally responsible for doing this and he will succeed if he is not stopped. The only way that we can stop him is from a distance, by sending electric shocks through him for an hour, deliberately controlling and gradating the level of pain so that it inhibits his movement.[9] This causes him great distress and temporarily incapacitates him until we can reach the pair.

A is completely defenseless with respect to our attacks on him, even while he is trying to attack B. Independent of whether doing this is permissible, the question is whether doing this is appropriately thought of as torturing someone in order to stop his attack. I think it is. If so it would involve torturing someone while he is a threat to B. Perhaps doing these things in this Killer Case is permissible because we are trying to stop someone when he is a serious threat to someone else, and torture is morally problematic only when this is not true. But my conceptual point is that permissible torture of those who are threats is still torture.

Restricting oneself to a conception of torture that would follow from considering only the cases Shue considers, in which the person tortured is defenseless and not a threat, would, I think, be an example of artificially narrowing the understanding of torture. Furthermore, narrowing the understanding of torture may result in capturing only cases where torture is morally impermissible or especially problematic. This comes close to defining torture as impermissible. Doing this may leave us no longer able to describe many instances of what should be considered torture as torture and unable to even coherently ask about torture *whether* it is always impermissible (if we define it as such).

Shue himself implicitly alters his initial characterization of torture, even as it occurs in the cases of interest to him. He considers that sometimes someone who refrains from giving information that could stop a threat might not be totally defenseless, for he has a way of "protecting himself from, and stopping the attack on him, by giving the information."[10] This could be true only when it is possible for the person to comply with the request for information (and Shue thinks the range of cases in which this is true is limited).[11] Hence, he thinks it is possible that some uses of torture do not involve victims who are defenseless. Notice that the defense imagined here is not counterattack but rather surrender. This is an unusual sense of "defense." It is like saying that a combatant can defend himself against an attack because if he surrenders the attack will stop.

(Shue distinguishes cases of interrogational torture that might allow for such self-protection from what he calls terroristic torture. In terroristic torture, someone is tortured in order to intimidate other people into doing something, so, he says, the person tortured cannot himself control whether the torture will end by giving information. It is not clear, however, that terroristic torture involves defenselessness, if having the aid of *others* in combating an attack on oneself can provide a defense. This is because even if the person tortured to intimidate other people has no control over them, it is possible that these other people may be intimidated and change their behavior out of concern for the tortured person. Indeed, they might do this even more rapidly than he would have divulged information he had. In this way, their actions can be a form of defense for him, given that torturing him will end when the others yield. Hence, it seems that even terroristic torture might not involve an attack on the defenseless. [Terroristic torture opens up the possibility, of course, that other people who are intimidated or pressured are being tortured psychologically, even though they are not defenseless to stop their being tortured.])

Suppose that Shue is correct to revise his account of torture as it actually occurs (and so as it is conceptually possible for it to occur) to include the possibility of torturing those who are not defenseless because they can surrender. (The possibility of such torture does not mean it is permissible.) We noted above, in discussing attacks on combatants in wartime, that the inability of someone to defend himself by counterattack did not seem relevant to whether he remained a combatant or to the permissibility of attacking him to stop his threats. The same would be true if this individual lacked the ability to defend himself by surrendering.[12] (For example, the combatant might lack the capacity to signal surrender.) So it is not clear that in the case of torture either, a person lacking the ability to protect himself (or the inability of others to protect him) by doing what is asked of him (or them) is what makes torture impermissible when it is impermissible.

B. SUSSMAN

Now let us consider Sussman's characterization of torture, with only minimal attention to the moral issues they raise. He says:

> At a minimum, torture involves the deliberate infliction of great pain or some other intensely distressing affective state (fear, shame, disgust, and so forth) on an unwilling person for purposes that person does not and could not reasonably be expected to share.... In addition... torture seems to require that its perpetrators and victims be

placed in a distinctive kind of social setting and relationship to one another. Victims of torture must be, and must realize themselves to be, completely at the mercy of their tormentors. This condition involves two distinct elements. First, being at another's mercy requires that there be a profoundly asymmetric relation of dependence and vulnerability between the parties. The victim of torture must be unable to shield herself in any significant way, and she must be unable to effectively evade or retaliate against her tormentor....

Second, the torture victim must see herself as being unable to put up any real moral or legal resistance to her tormentor. The victim takes her tormentor to be someone who can do anything he wants to her, who does not have to worry about answering any challenges that the victim (or her representatives) might put to him. The torturer confronts no moral or legal impediments stemming from his victim's will, but evidently takes himself to be limited only by his own desires and interests, or the desires and interests of those he serves as an agent....The asymmetry of power, knowledge, and prerogative is absolute: the victim is in a position of complete vulnerability and exposure, the torturer in one of perfect control and inscrutability.

Characteristically, the torture victim finds herself to be not only physically and morally defenseless, but [also] exposed to a will that appears largely if not completely arbitrary....Of course, a victim might know that she is being tortured for a specific purpose (to obtain some particular piece of information, perhaps, or to incriminate someone) or that her torturers operate under some significant restrictions (perhaps they have orders not to kill or leave any permanent marks on the victim). Yet even in these cases, the victim's only grounds for such beliefs about her tormentors' ends and intentions come from how these tormentors choose to present themselves to her. Typically, a torture victim has no independent way of corroborating any admissions or assurances of her torturers.[13]

Despite this characterization, Sussman does not think that torture, even in the cases he is most interested in, necessarily involves a victim who no longer presents a threat to anyone. I conclude this, in part, because he considers whether, even in *self-defense*, we might be more reluctant to torture someone than to kill him.[14] This conclusion is also supported by his views (a) that someone who refrains from giving information that could easily be given to stop a threat to innocents is maintaining the threat, and (b) that if this person also started the threat, it is appropriate to say that in maintaining the threat, he is still *presenting* the threat.[15]

Notice that for Shue, what is important about someone who could comply with a request to give information about the threat he started is that he is not defenseless (in the sense that he may have a means of stopping the torture). For Sussman, what is important about such a person is that he is maintaining and indeed still presenting a threat. If a person is still presenting a threat, then inflicting distress on him in order to stop his threat would not be a typical instance of torture on Shue's characterization of it. By contrast, inflicting distress on such a person is consistent with Sussman's characterization of torture.

Sussman thinks that interrogational torture has a distinctive wrong-making characteristic, though this does not, therefore, make it worse or a more serious wrong than other things we might do to someone. The distinctive wrong-making characteristic is supposed to involve taking over someone's body so that he is aware of his body and his sense of agency (insofar as it is intimately bodily) *betraying him* by "speaking" on behalf of the torturer. (This is not to be confused with a terrorist deciding to betray his cause by giving the information.) Sussman distinguishes between "collusion" between the tortured person's body and the torturer, which he calls "treachery" of the body, and mere "insubordination" of one's body when it is in pain due to illness. He thinks that pain always involves a plea for the pain to stop, but when one is tortured, it also involves one's body "speaking" for the torturer, asking one to give the torturer information so that pain will stop. One instinctively identifies with one's body's plea for pain to stop (whatever one decides to do on reflection). If one resists the plea, one will have the sense that one is oneself responsible for the pain because one might have stopped it by giving the information. And if one does not resist the plea and one does what the torturer wants, one is being brought to exercise one's agency on behalf of the torturer by one's body having been taken over.

Sussman considers such a psychological division of an agent brought on by torture a perversion of agency.[16] What seems to be particularly important on Sussman's account of torture is that torture aims at getting the tortured person *to act*—so it is coercive—and this coercion comes about though affecting his body (or affective states) (unlike a coercive threat to do something to someone later). Similarly distressing treatment that merely aims to *interfere with an act* that someone has chosen for himself or that aims at eliciting non-act responses from someone is not torture on Sussman's view.[17]

One of my concerns about Sussman's characterization of torture is that it leads to an attempt to inappropriately narrow our use of the term. It thus reduces the cases in which we could say that impermissible *torture* is taking place. Indeed, more than Shue, Sussman seems concerned with identifying a concept rather than merely characterizing common cases of torture. For example, Sussman's account of the distinctiveness of torture has the counterintuitive result that it is impossible to torture an animal if the animal is incapable of either seeing its body as being taken over by a person whose case it pleads or consciously exercising its agency on behalf of another.[18] Rather than saying that his account is not intended to capture all possible cases of torture, Sussman says of animals that he is willing to "bite this bullet."[19]

Similarly, suppose that we secretly infect someone with a virus that causes him extreme pain for a long period of time as a means of getting him to blurt out information (or make information-revealing jerking movements) while he suffers. I believe that we are torturing the person though the person (a) does not believe we are trying to affect him through his body, and (b) he does not yield the information by being coerced into action. He only believes he is ill and that his body is "insubordinate" not in collusion with another agent, and he only babbles information in a disoriented frame of mind (or jerks uncontrollably). Hence, on Sussman's account, doing this to someone is not torture. Nor does Sussman think that punishing someone with extreme pain is torture. He calls such punishments "ordeals," because there is nothing for the victim to do but just take it, by contrast to interrogational torture, where the victim thinks his revealing information might change how things go. Sussman's account, therefore, also rules out Shue's class of "terroristic torture" as really an instance of physical torture.

If this account of Sussman's views is correct, then Killer Case (1), which I presented as a case in which we torture someone who is a threat, will also not involve torture in Sussman's view. This is because we are simply making it impossible for A to carry out his attack by continuously sending incapacitating and painful shocks.[20] While I think that Killer Case (1) *is* a case of torture, it is important to see that we could construct a variant on it that satisfies Sussman's criteria because it involves getting A to act by coercive violence. In Killer Case (2), the only way to stop A's attack on B is to use the same form of painful treatment of his body when it does not directly stop his attack or elicit mere movements not under A's control. Rather the painful treatment must lead to A's cooperating agency, as in interrogational torture. In this case, A is completely defenseless relative to us (while he is actively presenting a threat to B). We make him suffer intensely for an hour by using a device long distance that causes him controlled and gradated pain when he knows that we are doing this to him in order to get him to decide to refrain from setting his bomb to go off. The pain is not directly incapacitating, for he could try to resist its effects and continue to set the bomb. We are just trying to get him to give in, he might hope to stop the torture by giving in, and his doing this will indeed stop the torture. I think getting him to refrain is getting him to do something in the sense in which Sussman is concerned with action. But we could also imagine that A is about to press button Y that will set off the bomb and the only way to stop him is to get him to press button X instead (or to say a code that triggers the voice-activated button X). (Pressing the button is a positive act.) The only way to get him to press button X is to affect his body in the same way, until he decides to stop resisting and press it. If A gives in and presses X to stop the pain, this will also make pressing Y ineffective as a means of setting off the bomb. (We could also vary the cases so that the effect on his body is humiliating; for example, it causes him to defecate. He could stop our causing this effect by stopping his threatening acts or by doing an alternative act.)

(As noted, Sussman thinks that "characteristically" the torture victim experiences being exposed to the unrestricted and seemingly arbitrary will of another. Hence, he may not think that this feature is part of the concept of torture. He says the victim might "know" that her torturers operate under restrictions, "yet even in these cases, the victim's only grounds for such beliefs...come from how the tormenters...present themselves." It seems odd to think that if these are only grounds for the victim's beliefs, that he could have "knowledge" about restrictions. But it is possible that a victim has general knowledge, independent of the torturers, of their religious beliefs or conceptions of honor. He could then know that they take seriously the prohibitions on doing certain things to him. If being exposed to an unrestricted will were taken as definitive of torture, then, given knowledge on the victim's part about restrictions, no matter what horrible acts his captors did to him, the victim would not be tortured. Such narrowing of the concept of torture would be incorrect, I believe.)

CONCLUSION

In light of this discussion of Shue and Sussman, I shall henceforth distinguish between "torture-wide" and "torture-narrow." Torture-wide can involve physical or psychological distress to either directly *interfere* with someone's act (e.g., by incapacitating him) *or* to elicit behavior not under someone's control (as in a case where the tortured person will reveal information or behave in a way that stops his threatening act by jerking or babbling). (Hence, torture-wide can apply to making people perform, in a broad sense of "perform," not only to directly interfering with their act.) Torture-narrow involves physical or psychological distress to get someone to decide to do an act under his control, and so tries to affect his will and get him to perform an action (not merely behave or move). It is coercive in the Kantian sense. Since torture-wide can cause people to perform (in a broad sense), the noncoercive/coercive distinction does not coincide with the interference/performance distinction. (In an inclusive rather than contrasting sense, torture-wide would include torture-narrow as a subpart, but I shall use it in a contrasting sense. This most inclusive sense of torture would come close to "the intentional and direct infliction of severe mental or physical suffering" [as in the *OED*].) I take Killer Case (1) to be an instance of torture-wide and Killer Case (2) to be an instance of torture-narrow.[21]

An even narrower notion of torture—"supernarrow"—would make reference to other narrowing features, such as the absence of known restrictions on torturers and the absence of defensive shields had by captives. It is important to realize that narrowing the conception of torture can be part of attempts by governments to find a way of permitting certain things to be done to captives while agents strictly avoid the charge of torture. For example, suppose those who control captives were restricted by laws requiring oversight by independent authorities, and defense lawyers were assigned to captives. Then even if those who control captives treat them brutally, they would not have, or be thought to have, an "unrestricted will." Hence, they might evade the charge of torturing in a supernarrow sense, even though most people would correctly still consider their acts to be torture.[22]

II. *Torture During an Act to Stop the Act*

Let us now focus on normative issues, including whether torture is worse than other prima facie (or pro tanto) wrongs, and whether it is always impermissible to torture someone, in particular because of what it does to the person tortured.[23] I shall begin by considering cases where torture might be used to directly stop an agent's harmful act (i.e., torture-wide).

A. SUBSTITUTING A LESSER, "MORALLY DIRTY," EVIL FOR A GREATER EVIL

Consider Killer Case (3): A is about to set off a bomb in order to kill innocent, nonthreatening B. A is morally responsible for doing this, and he will succeed if he is not stopped. There are only two ways to stop A. One way is to kill him. I shall assume that it would be permissible to do this if it were the only way to stop him.[24] The only alternative is to torture A for an hour in the manner described in Killer Case (1) involving torture-wide, making it physically impossible for him to set off the bomb.[25] Is substituting torturing A for killing him permissible (or even obligatory)? I believe it is at least permissible. One possible explanation of this is that we can still accomplish the goal of saving B by attacking A and also act in A's interests by torturing rather than killing, because being tortured for an hour is much less bad for A than being killed.[26]

Let us consider this explanation. First, in what sense is it less bad for A to be tortured than to be killed? After all, it may be said, many would reasonably prefer to be killed than to undergo torture. I agree. However, this would probably be true only if the torture were of a different type or lasted for far longer than an hour, as I have described it in this case. Periods of comparable pain (that are not torture) are often reasonably endured (e.g., in medical procedures) to avoid death. Even though death does not involve experienced suffering, it involves the loss of all goods of life, and this can be worse for someone than a period of suffering.[27] However, I have no easy formula for deciding when something is less bad than being killed (or death). In particular, nothing I say commits me to an overall utility (or, more generally, consequentialist) calculation, according to which so long as a period of torture would be followed by a life worth living whose positive value is greater than the negative value of the torture, then torture, rather than death, is in the interest of the person tortured. Indeed, when discussing painful medical treatments given to the so-called Texas Burn Victim patient, I have suggested that some stretch of painful experiences could be so bad that it is not unreasonable to exercise a prerogative not to go through it, even to get to a life whose positive value would be much greater than the negative value of the pain experienced.[28] Hence, even though it has been said that consequentialist calculations are suitable for making decisions intrapersonally (even if not interpersonally), I do not assume this is true.[29]

Some may argue that it is *part of torture* that its victim does not know that it will *not* go on interminably, and so, perhaps, be worse than being killed.[30] I believe that this is another way of narrowing the understanding of torture; it implies that if A were truthfully told and believed that our painfully shocking him would last for only an hour, we could not be engaged in torturing him. I do not think this is true. However, let us suppose that A is given no grounds for believing that the torture will *not* go on indefinitely, and that A's believing that the pain will not end is itself a bad thing for him. We then have to consider whether his having an episode of pain that (we know) will stop in an hour *in conjunction with* his (incorrect) belief that it will not end, could still be much less bad for A than his being killed. I think it could be. Hence, even if we should take into account the beliefs of the victim to determine how bad the episode is for him, it is a mistake to take his subjective perspective at face value. That is, it is a mistake in deciding how bad the painful episode is for him by comparison with death, to treat his belief that the pain may never end as true.[31]

Sussman, for one, does not believe that torture, even in the case of torture-narrow, is necessarily worse for someone than being deprived of his life. I think evidence for this is that he says that he is not arguing that third parties should choose to stop an innocent person from being tortured rather than stop another innocent person from being killed.

So, let us now assume that torture-wide in Killer Case (3) is better for A than his being killed. How does this bear on (a) how reluctant one should be to torture rather than kill and (b) whether it is permissible to torture rather than kill? As noted above, Sussman says that even in self-defense, one could appropriately be "more *reluctant* to torture someone than to kill him" (p. 8) (where I take it he is referring to torture-narrow). So, he seems to believe that we should be more reluctant to treat someone in a way that is better for him than in a way that is worse for him. This is often true; for example, we could appropriately be more reluctant to treat someone paternalistically (for his own good, but contrary to his will and values) than to let him make his own mistakes. We could be more reluctant to tell someone an unpleasant truth that is better for him to know than to let him be harmfully deluded.

However, I think that even Sussman, if he accepted that A would be tortured in Killer Case (3), could agree that it is permissible to torture A rather than kill him in this case. This is not only because what is involved is torture-wide, but because in Killer Case (3), it is not true that a person is being tortured "for purposes that a person does not and could not reasonably be expected to share" (p. 9).[32] Arguably, in Killer Case (3), A is wide-tortured, in part, for purposes he could reasonably be expected to share, that is, his not being killed. In addition, whether we do what is better (torture) or worse (kill) for A, we will be acting contrary to his expressed will. This contrasts with doing something that is better for someone when we have his permission only to do something else that is, in fact, less good for him. In this case, we would override someone's will (paternalistically) only when we do something better; we can avoid it entirely if we do what is less good for him. In our Killer Cases, however, we already assume it is permissible to kill contrary to the wrongdoer's will. Hence, it is possible that (i) when whatever we do will be contrary to someone's will, (ii) we are at liberty to do what is much better for him because his own good is a purpose he could reasonably be expected to share.[33]

It may be objected that factors (i) and (ii) are insufficient to justify torture rather than killing, as shown by the fact that it is morally impermissible to enslave people as the alternative to killing them.[34]

Note, however, that the context in which the choice between the latter two options is ordinarily present involves deciding whether to (a) win a war by killing one's opponent or (b) win it in some other way and then enslave one's opponent permanently. However, for a war case to be analogous to the Killer Cases, it would have to involve forcing people to labor as the *only way to win the war that does not involve permissibly killing them.* So imagine that if we do not kill our opponents, the only way to win the war is to keep them busy working for us against their will for a few months. That is, if they stop laboring in this way and are not killed, they will win the war. I submit that in this sort of case, it would be permissible to force labor rather than to kill. By contrast, the ordinary context in which enslaving rather than killing is discussed does not involve a short period of forced labor as the only alternative to permissibly killing as a means to winning a war. Rather, it involves forcing labor for our postwar convenience, and just as killing people for our convenience after we have won a war against them is not permissible, longterm forced labor once we have won a war is not permissible either.

It seems, therefore, that the view that it is impermissible to do something bad as the alternative to killing, even when this is greatly in the interest of those who suffer, is often based on an incomplete consideration of cases. That is, the view is not based on considering cases where all factors besides killing and the alternative to it are kept constant. For example, it seems to be based on comparing cases where killing itself is necessary to win a war but forced labor itself is not necessary to win a war.[35] If temporary forced labor could be permissible as the alternative to killing to win a war, this supports the permissibility of some torture rather than killing to stop a killer. However, our further discussion does show that the facts that (i') being tortured and being killed are both contrary to someone's will and (ii') being tortured rather than being killed far better serves purposes someone could reasonably be expected to share are not sufficient to make some torture rather than killing permissible unless (iii) the torture serves the same purpose that the permissible killing would serve, not necessarily when it serves very different purposes. (Hence, [i] and [ii] [as described on p. 17] must also be supplemented by [iii]: What is much better serves the same purpose as would be served by what is worse.)[36]

In personal communication, Sussman (with whose permission I quote) says in response to Killer Case (3):

> I agree that here it might be morally preferable to torture A than to kill him. My claim though was that it doesn't seem to be morally confused or the mark of bad character to feel a greater reluctance to torture than to kill, even if this doesn't correspond to the morally correct decision here.... Part of what I'm trying to get at is the sense that torture, while perhaps permissible, is inherently 'dirty' in a way that killing isn't, even though a dirty act may sometimes be morally preferable to a more clean one. (Call this Quote 1.)

Suppose Sussman is correct and that a greater reluctance to torture need not correspond to the morally correct decision. Then if we are concerned with whether torture could sometimes be morally permissible, as I am in this discussion, we may not get much guidance from a consideration and in-depth analysis of its special "dirty" character.

(Interestingly, though Killer Case [3] does not involve torture-narrow, Sussman did not object to its being a case of torture in his communication. Furthermore, his remarks about its sometimes being morally preferable to do a dirty act than a clean one, clearly may also apply to torture-narrow, which he identified with torture in his article.)

Now consider how what Sussman says in Quote 1 compares with what he says about his not arguing that it is worse for someone to be tortured than to be killed (in the following quote). He says (in personal communication), repeating published views of his to which I have partly already referred:

> I'm not making a comparison of harms, prior to the particular relation someone stands in toward the situation. The special strength of the reason against torturing may not translate into a similar, especially strong reason to prevent tortures (that is, especially strong relative to the reason to prevent killings or maimings, say). (Call this Quote 2.)

Quote 2 is consistent with the view that it would be *wrong* for an agent to torture A rather than kill him (because there is a reason of "special strength" against torturing), even though there is no reason of special strength to prevent tortures rather than killings. By contrast, Quote 1 implies that there might be *no* reason of special *strength* against torturing (by comparison to killing), only a reason of a special *quality* which can make us more reluctant to torture and mislead us as to its relative strength. It is the latter position that is closer to the truth, I think, and that Sussman says he accepts, at least in Killer Case (3), where he says it is morally preferable to torture than to kill.

As already noted, the torture imagined in Killer Cases (1) and (3) are not instances of torture-narrow, as described by Sussman, for the pain we cause directly incapacitates A. I think it is useful to show that the difference between torture-wide and torture-narrow need not affect the moral permissibility of torturing A instead of killing him, though it can raise new issues. So we should consider Killer Case (4), which is like Killer Case (2) except that it is physically possible to kill A instead of using torture-narrow in order to stop his attack on B. It is still permissible, I think, to substitute torture-narrow for killing from concern for A himself. This is true, even though we aim to directly affect his agency by physical means only in torture-narrow.

But what if A would prefer to be killed rather than (predictably) act to betray his important mission of killing B just to stop the torture, when it does not directly incapacitate him? Betraying his cause to stop the torture may be a fate that, given his values, he would regard as worse than death.[37] Given his values and assuming he will give in, it does not seem that he could reasonably share the purpose of torturing rather than killing him. If we know all this about him, in what sense could it still be permissible for us to narrow-torture A rather than kill him in order to save B, out of concern for A himself?[38]

Perhaps it is helpful in thinking about some aspects of this case to recall Thomas Scanlon's discussion, in his article "Preference and Urgency,"[39] of the person who would prefer to have aid from us to build a monument to his god rather than to save him from starvation. His service to his god is more important to him than his own life. Nevertheless, Scanlon argues, it is his nutritional, not his religious, interests that he has a claim on us to consider in deciding to aid him. This is so even though, given his values, it does not seem that he could reasonably share the purpose of feeding him rather than helping build the monument. In Killer Case (4), where we are concerned with how we shall harm someone rather than how we shall aid him, I believe that A has no claim on us to kill him rather than narrow-torture him to save B, even though his values lead him to prefer the former. This might be because the interest of his that he has a claim on us to consider is his survival, whose value does not depend on his personal conception of it, rather than the protection of his honor whose value, like the value of a monument to one's god, depends on his conception of it. (Yet, it might also be permissible of us to avoid killing A and rather subject him to torture whose humiliating nature does not depend on A's personal conception of it. So, what may be important is that A's view that humiliating torture has greater disvalue than death depends on his personal conception, and that need have no hold on us.[40]) We need not kill A rather than torture him just so that he does not, as he sees it, dishonorably betray his cause in order to avoid torture.

If A would find his betraying his goal of killing B in order to make torture stop a fate worse than death, he would also presumably find it even more shameful to betray his goal because we successfully tempt him to refrain (or to perform some other act) with luxury, food, or money. (This could be so, whether he gives in to the mere prospect of such goods while in complete control of himself or he succumbs to their undermining his self-control when they are actually present and felt.) Yet stopping A's act by the temptations could still be morally permissible and preferable to killing him. In general, it is often morally preferable to prompt someone to act badly or to oneself engage in conduct that humiliates him rather than to kill or severely harm him, even when the latter would be permissible were there no alternative.[41]

It seems then that even if, given his values, someone could not reasonably share our purpose in torturing him rather than killing him, it could be permissible to torture him against his will rather than kill him against his will, when torturing accomplishes what killing would have, because doing this better serves those interests of the aggressor that he has a claim on us to consider.

As noted earlier, Shue thinks that it should be possible for someone who would be tortured for information to comply with the request for information. He thinks that this condition is not fulfilled if someone would have to betray a cause to which he is sincerely committed. In general, he thinks that the choice we offer someone should not be between what that person sees as two evils (e.g., his being tortured or his betraying his cause). Hence, he thinks that it is impermissible to torture someone, even if, considered independently of the aggressor's values, the alternative of betrayal is a lesser evil for the person than being tortured. In Killer Case (4), however, it is assumed that it would be permissible to kill A, if this were the only way to stop his killing B. So the permissibility of killing A does not depend on A being able to do something to avoid being killed that is not a "mere lesser evil." Hence, even if we accepted Shue's views on when compliance is "possible" to avoid the *greater* evil of torture, this need not imply that our choosing between what is otherwise a permissible greater evil (killing) and the lesser evil of torture is impermissible.

It is possible that in the cases Shue considers, he thinks we must offer more than a choice between evils, not because a choice between evils offers no possibility of compliance, but because compliance *is* possible. That is, he may be concerned that if someone *does* comply by choosing the lesser evil of giving in, we will have helped him do a morally shameful act (betray his cause). Shue may think we should not do this. This would be a different ground for objecting to torturing rather than killing, namely that we are trying to get someone to do something shameful in getting him to betray his cause to avoid torture. By contrast, being killed is not shameful. But as the case of permissible temptation by pleasure (raised in the text above) shows, this objection fails.[42]

In sum, if it is permissible to kill someone against his will as he attacks, for example, on grounds of other-defense, and this permissible act would have been done, then it may also be permissible to torture that person for the same purpose, on the grounds that at least some ways of torturing a person are much less bad for him than the killing that would have taken place. More generally, if it is permissible to do something seriously harmful to a person against his will and one would have done it, then it may sometimes be permissible to do something much less harmful instead, holding constant the purpose for which it is done and the manner in which the harm is imposed (for example, direct attack).[43]

B. THE "DIRTY EVIL" ON ITS OWN

Now return to Killer Cases (1) and (2), which are like Killer Cases (3) and (4) in all respects except that one is not physically able to kill A, though it would be permissible to do so if it were physically possible and necessary to stop A's attack. It is, in fact, only physically possible to torture (wide or narrow) A to stop his attack. Is it permissible to torture? Since there would be no exchange of (a) death for (b) temporary torture, it might be said that torture no longer serves a purpose that its victim could reasonably share nor does it serve an interest of his that has a claim on us. However, if it would be *permissible* to kill A in defense of B were it physically possible and necessary, then presumably one should be able to do A a lesser harm, such as paralyzing his leg in defense of B. Does this imply that one may torture A to interfere with his act?

It might be argued (to repeat what was said above) that torture—especially torture-narrow—is not merely a lesser harm. It is "dirty." As Sussman tries to argue, torture-narrow, at least, is qualitatively different from shooting someone in the leg, in a way that would make one reluctant to do it to someone, even when one would not be similarly reluctant to shoot him in the leg. In particular, it might be said that one should not torture A in Killer Cases (1) and (2), because A's killing B would not involve the particularly repulsive features of torturing A (wide or narrow).

Is this argument available to someone who agrees that in Killer Cases (3) and (4), it would be permissible to torture A rather than cause *his* own death to save B? That is, it might be said that if it is permissible to exchange the nonrepulsive killing of A for the repulsive torture of A, for A's own sake, so long as it also saves B's life, then the mere fact that the nonrepulsive killing of B will be exchanged for the *repulsive* torture of A should not stand in the way of torturing A. After all, if saving B's life is more important than not taking A's life, and not taking A's life is more important than not torturing A, then should not saving B also be more important than not torturing A? In essence, this conclusion depends on the following transitivity argument: (1) X (saving B's life from A's attack) takes precedence over Y (not killing A), (2) Y (not killing A) takes precedence over Z (not torturing A), hence (3) X (saving B's life from A's attack) takes precedence over Z (not torturing A).

This transitivity argument definitely does *not* imply that it is always permissible to do a less harmful act that is one's only option just because one may permissibly do it as a substitute when another more harmful permissible act is also available.[44] For it may be crucial how a harm to someone comes about and/or what its role is. These factors may make doing the less harmful act wrong when it is one's only option, even though not wrong when it substitutes for a different, permissible way of bringing about greater harm. For example, it seems to be permissible to turn a trolley away from killing five people, even though it then kills one other person on another track. However, it is not permissible to topple a person in front of the trolley so that he stops it, even though this would only paralyze him, when this is the only way to save the five. The way in which he comes to be harmed in the first case (e.g., as a consequence of a redirection of a threat) seems to make the greater harm permissible by contrast to the way the lesser harm comes about in the second case. However, it would be permissible, I think, to topple the person in front of the trolley so that he stops it when this only paralyzes him, as a substitute for otherwise killing him by redirecting the trolley. The constraint on bringing about harm to a person in a certain way can sometimes be overridden when it is in his own interest to be treated in that way, given that the permissible alternative would make him worse off.[45]

In Killer Cases (1) and (2), however, the way we bring about the lesser harm does not differ from the way we would bring about a greater harm. More precisely, the way in which we would cause the lesser harm (paralyzing the killer's leg or torturing him) *and* the role of the lesser harm as a means to stop his attack are the same as the way in which we would (if possible) cause the greater harm (death of the killer) and the role of the greater harm. (That is, we would kill him by an act that serves no other morally permissible function and employs him as a means to stop his attack.) This is one reason why, given that killing would be permissible if necessary, causing the lesser harm could be permissible, *even when it is one's only option* in Killer Cases (1) and (2).

Assume that a difference in how the lesser and greater harms would be brought does not stand in the way of permissibly torturing when it is necessary to stop A from killing. There is still another possible problem with the transitivity argument. The argument depends on the idea that it is the relative importance of saving B and not killing A that bears on whether one may torture A to save B, if one may torture A rather than kill him to save B. That is, it says that if one may torture to save a life whose continuation is less significant in this context, then one may torture to save the life whose continuation is more significant in this context. But this argument fails to consider that the life whose continuation is less significant in this context (A's) may have a property which the life whose continuation is more significant in this context (B's) does not have, and it is in virtue of *that* property that we may torture A. This property is that it is A's *own life* that will be saved if he is tortured (regardless of how relatively insignificant the continuation of his life is in this context). This is a personal rather than an impersonal consideration (such as the relative significance, in the context, of each person's life continuing) and it does not support torturing A for B's sake. This counterargument suggests that we may only do something "dirty" (torture-wide or -narrow) for the good of the person tortured; we cannot conclude that dirty harms may be done when they are our only option just because greater nondirty harms may be done when they are our only option.

Consider, however, that it may be important that torture saves A's own life because he cares about his life. This suggests that if A cared as much about his potential victim B's life as he cares about his own life, there would be fewer problems with the transitivity argument. What if A does not care about his own life (e.g., he is unreasonably suicidal)? It might be permissible to torture him rather than kill him, because (i) he *should* care about his own life, and (ii) his interests are served by being tortured rather than killed. If the fact that he should care about his own life licenses torture as a substitute for killing, this raises the possibility of arguing that he *should* care to save his potential victim's life as much as or more than he should care to save his own life. (A person who realized that he had done something morally wrong that would kill someone and now wanted to do the right thing would, presumably, give up his own life to save his victim if this were necessary.) If so, it might be suggested, the transitivity argument could be revised to hold that if we may torture A for the sake of one thing he should care about to a high degree, then we may torture him for the sake of another thing he should care about to the same (or even higher) degree. But notice that there are two different senses of "should" involved: (1) the should of reasonable prudence in the case of caring for his own life, and (2) the should of moral obligation towards his potential victim. Hence, the argument might have to be supplemented with an intermediate claim, for example, that it would be morally wrong to place greater importance on considerations of prudence than those of moral obligation to one's victim (in the case we are considering).⁴⁶

Now suppose, contrary to fact, that killing A would be morally *imper-missible* in Killer Cases (1)–(4). Suppose also that it is the size of the loss to A, not the way it comes about or its role (e.g., as a causal means to saving a victim) that makes killing impermissible. It might still be permissible to cause A lesser harms to stop his attack on B, and even "dirty" harm involved in torturing him, when this is one's only option. Whether one may do this might be decided by a direct proportionality calculation. That is, we ask, how much less of a cost than death would it be permissible to impose to stop A's killing B. The direct proportionality calculation could also be used to decide whether torturing A is permissible if killing *would* be permissible if necessary. Alternatively, one might proceed indirectly: Suppose that a direct proportionality calculation implied that it was permissible to shoot A in the leg, even though it would permanently paralyze it, in order to stop his killing B. Then we could consider whether it would be permissible to substitute torturing him (to the degree imagined in Killer Cases [1]–[4]), for shooting his leg in order to save B. If such a substitution would be permissible because it was consistent with his interests, then we might try to use the transitivity arguments suggested earlier and argue for the permissibility of torturing him in order to save B when we are physically unable to shoot him in the leg.

At this point, I believe we can conclude that it is sometimes permissible to torture someone, at least for a short period without permanent damage, if we *would* otherwise permissibly kill him. It is not clear that it follows *straightforwardly* from this that it is permissible to torture someone in this way for a goal whenever it would be permissible (though not actually possible) to kill him for that goal. Nevertheless, I have suggested that there are grounds for believing this too would be permissible.

C. JUSTIFICATIONS FOR PERMISSIBLE AND OBLIGATORY TORTURE

1. *Permissible Torture and Moral Innocents.* So far, I have mostly presented intuitive judgments about cases and implications we might draw from some cases for others. However, in (B), I pointed to one approach to justifying these judgments: In virtue of his acts, A owes it to his potential victim to (at least) stop his acts, even at the cost of his own life. If he does not do this, he is liable to being killed or tortured by others to stop his acts. Being liable in this way need not always imply that *an agent owes it to his victim* to allow himself to be killed or tortured, or that he owes it to his victim to give up his life or to torture himself, if this were (somehow possible and) necessary to stop his killing his victim. One could become liable to being attacked in order to stop one's acts, even if one did not have these other obligations. For example, suppose a pilot in a just war will be permissibly bombing a munitions factory despite the collateral deaths of noncombatants. He is doing nothing morally wrong and is not in a morally inappropriate position. Yet, arguably, in virtue of his threatening acts he is liable to being permissibly killed by those noncombatants themselves in their attempt to stop his doing what will kill them. (They are not merely excused in doing this, but justified.)[47] If they could stop him by torturing him (as in the Killer Cases) at a distance, and this is much better for him than death, it seems permissible for them to do this, too. May third parties also attack the pilot in defense of the noncombatants? Arguably, their compatriots could permissibly do this. However, his being liable to this attack in virtue of his acts need not, I believe, imply (1) that he has an obligation to the bystanders to bomb the munitions factory in a way that will cause his death instead of the bystanders', or (2) that it is impermissible for him to stop the bystanders from killing him by shooting back at them.

However, in Killer Cases (1)–(4), I believe, one of the reasons A is liable to being killed or tortured to save B is that he actually owes it to B to allow these things to be done to him, or to do them to himself, in order to stop his attack on B.[48] This is because he, unlike the pilot, is responsible for doing something seriously morally wrong. There is a difficulty, however, in arguing that he is liable to *our* killing or torturing him for B's sake simply on grounds of what he owes B, for it is not, in general, true that when A owes B something, third parties may either force him to fulfill his obligation or impose a cost on him that results in B getting what is owed to him. Yet I think that sometimes doing these things is permissible, and the Killer Cases are instances of this. I shall not pursue these issues further here, but they do need to be pursued to complete an argument.

2. *Obligatory Torture and Moral Innocents.* So far, my arguments have concerned the *permissibility* of torturing in the Killer Cases. But if it is permissible to torture A to stop his killing B, might it not also some-times be *obligatory* for a public official charged with the safety of the public to torture A to stop A killing B? Perhaps it is permissible but not required for such an official to torture A when that is the only thing he could do to stop A from killing B, because it is a repulsive task for the agent to do the torturing—it may be too much to demand of *him* that he do this. The act would be supererogatory. (I am distinguishing between [i] the repulsiveness or psychological burden of torturing for the torturer and [ii] the torture being morally wrong. It can be repulsive even if it is morally permissible.)[49]

However, in cases where the public official is permitted to kill and would do so, might he be *required* to torture instead of kill, though torturing is psychologically harder for him? To answer this question, it may help to consider a killer case in which A is going to shoot B but A is a morally innocent threat. For example, someone has hypnotized him to do this wrongful killing. Suppose, as many think, it is still per-missible to kill A if necessary to stop his killing B, but we are able to torture him instead (to the degree described in previous cases). I sus-pect that the willingness to do the psychologically burdensome tortur-ing increases as A's moral innocence increases, because we are more willing to act out of concern for saving A's life when he is morally inno-cent than when he is morally guilty. A further test of this conclusion is to imagine that a fully responsible, morally guilty A says that unless we torture B (in the manner we have imagined), A will kill him. If this is necessary to save innocent and nonthreatening B, we may well be more willing to do the burdensome torturing than in order to save A in our earlier cases. This is so, even though from a moral point of view, tortur-ing B is less justified per se than torturing A (as B has done nothing that makes him liable to being tortured).

Consideration of this case suggests that if a public official is obligated to take seriously the interests of guilty aggressors (consistent with stopping their crimes), she should do for A what she would do for morally innocent B. Consideration of this case also shows that it might sometimes be morally permissible to torture morally innocent and nonthreatening persons.

D. UNCERTAINTY

In Killer Cases (1)–(4), I have been assuming that we know that A is trying to kill B, he will succeed if we do not stop him, and our acting will succeed in stopping him. However, it could be permissible for proper authorities to kill A if this was their only way of stopping A's attack, even if they were not completely certain (a) that A is trying to kill B, and/or (b) that he will succeed in killing him, and/or (c) that their killing A will save B. For example, it is *possible* that A is only pretending to be trying to kill B, and so he is using a nonworking gun. Or, it is possible that unbeknownst to A (who is trying to kill B) and to us, he has a nonworking gun. Further, our bullet might reach and kill A only after he sets off his gun. A policeman would not need to be absolutely certain of (a), (b), and (c) in order for it to be permissible for him to kill A.

Suppose we knew that A was trying to kill B but had *serious* doubts about whether he would succeed, because we have some (nonconclusive) evidence that the gun is nonworking. If we are certain that he is trying to kill B, I think that serious doubts about his being successful should have less effect on our decision to kill A to save B than if we also had serious doubts about whether he is trying to kill B.[50] Jeff McMahan argues similarly and offers the following explanation: Someone's moral guilt licenses imposing greater risks on him because the guilty party must bear the costs of creating a situation in which we are, in fact, uncertain what must be done in order to make sure that his victim will not die.[51]

If all this is true about killing A, then given what has been previously argued, it should also be true about torturing A to interfere with his act of killing B. Indeed, if torturing A is much less bad for him than being killed, an even higher level of uncertainty about (a), (b), and (c) may be consistent with the permissibility of torturing A to stop his act of attacking B than with the permissibility of killing A.

E. HUMAN RIGHTS

Suppose the intuitive judgments about the permissibility of torture in the Killer Cases are justified. This would show that while there may be a *human right* not to be tortured in the sense that one has only to be a human being (or a person) in order to *come to have* such a right, one might, through one's acts, come to lose or weaken the force of this right. Then one would remain a human being but lack the right not to be tortured in certain ways for certain purposes. (Alternatively, it may be said that it is not a matter of a right being lost or weakened. Rather, it is a matter of the specification of what the right not to be tortured, never lost or weakened, entails when one is attacking others and one's act can be stopped.[52])

However, it may be only for the sake of saving his victim that it is permissible to torture the wrongdoer to stop his act. According to one justification of torture that we have considered, this is because the weakening (or specification) of the right not to be tortured represents the subordination of considerations that support such a right to the obligation a wrongdoer has to his victim to suffer losses in order to stop his attack. The wrongdoer does not acquire such obligations to others who are not his victims. According to this proposed justification, it is such an obligation that underlies the right of others to torture the wrongdoer in order to stop his act of killing his victim.

CONCLUSION

For any type of torture that could be done to someone held captive *after* he has committed an act that *will* kill a victim unless we do something, we can imagine a hypothetical case in which the same torture could be applied to someone as he is in the process of attacking a victim. So we could take each of the forms of torture ruled out by international conventions on torture and imagine it being done to someone in the course of his attacking others in order to either interfere with his act or to lead him to decide to act differently. This would help us decide if any of these forms of torture could ever actually be morally permissible. It seems reasonable to think that if it would be permissible to kill someone to stop his act, it would be permissible to engage in some kinds of torture to interfere with his act or to get him to act differently, even if it leads to some permanent harm (e.g., his hand is paralyzed). Even if it were not permissible to kill him, some kinds of torture could still be proportional to stopping his act. This includes the hour of painful shocking I have described. It could also include this attacker being made to stand for many hours without sleep (treatment prohibited by international conventions) if only this will successfully stop his killing someone (by interfering with his act or by getting him to decide to stop attacking). The general argumentative strategy is to find the least harmful type of treatment that would still be considered torture. If it could permissibly be done to stop someone from killing, then torture is sometimes permissible. This argument, I believe, shows that if it is *not* correct to restrict the notion of torture so that it applies only to what is done to someone after he acts while held captive, some torture could be morally permissible.[53] Our discussion also shows that the question of whether some torture is sometimes permissible bears on the use of sublethal weapons during the apprehension of criminals and in war.

Furthermore, what I have argued implies that a wrongdoer may have no right not to be tortured even when he threatens only *one person* with death. (Indeed, we might sometimes be justified in torturing *several* people in order to frustrate their jointly killing only *one* person, as David Sussman has pointed out.[54] This is suggested by the fact that we could permissibly *kill* several people to stop their wrongfully killing one victim.) Hence, it seems that we need not imagine cases where the lives of thousands of people are at stake (as in typical "ticking bomb" scenarios) in order to justify torture.[55] However, if what I have argued is true, it would also be permissible to torture-wide or -narrow a terrorist during his act in order to stop his act of killing many people.

Hence, we cannot explain why torture is wrong in the many cases when it is done to people held captive by pointing to the characteristics shared by all torture just in virtue of being torture.[56]

III. *Torture During an Act to Stop the Act's Effects*

So far, I have been discussing what may be *done to someone during his act* of attacking *to stop his act*. I have considered interfering with the act directly or getting the agent to refrain or do another act on his own.[57] However, it is possible that other things could be done to someone during his act that do not stop the act itself but either (a) stop the success of the attack or (b) save the victim from harm despite the attack. We should consider whether such interventions, assuming they are the only way to stop the harm to the victim, are morally permissible.

A. BENEFICIAL USE OF A WRONGDOER DURING HIS ACT

Consider the second possibility (b) in Killer Case (5): A attacks B and will kill him unless we intervene. We cannot stop A's attack itself; we can only drop a protective mantle around B, which will save him from injury. The only way to make the mantle drop around B is to deliberately hit A with a bullet precisely as he successfully shoots his bullet at B. The bullet does not interfere with A's act but will cause his death shortly thereafter and his being dead causes the mantle to drop.

Here we deliberately do something to A that will shortly kill him while he is attacking B in order to prevent his harming B. It is permissible (in Killer Cases [3] and [4]) to kill A as he acts, in order to *stop his act and the attack* on B, at least in part because this will prevent harm to B that A would cause. (Presumably it would be wrong to kill A to stop his act when we [but not A] know that there is no way B can be harmed by A's act.) If this is so, then it seems that we should be permitted to do something to A as he is attacking B that will later kill A, in order to prevent his harming B, even if we must stop the harm in some way other than by stopping A's act. Suppose we may permissibly act in Killer Case 5 for this reason. Then it is not only to stop his wrong act that we may kill A.

Another way to prevent harm to B from A's attack involves a device that saves B even further along in the course of the attack. Suppose A attacks B by shooting up at him so that B will fall from a great height and die. We cannot stop A's attack or the fall; but hitting A with our bullet during his act will shortly kill him, causing a cushioning device to move into the spot where B will land, thus saving B. Intuitively, doing this seems permissible.[58]

Now consider the first possibility (a) by imagining the following variation on Killer Case (5) in which we can stop the attack on B but not A's act itself. In this variation, we can activate a screen in front of A that will prevent his bullet from traveling at all. The only way to activate the screen in front of A is to deliberately shoot him precisely as he shoots at B. A will shortly die, causing the screen to fall. Given what else we may do to A, it seems to me to be morally permissible to do this.

Possibly these cases involve using A to aid B, even though they also stop A from harming B. Let me explain. As we cannot stop A from acting, we do things to him that might also physically be done to any bystander who does not threaten B, in order to help protect B. That is, killing a bystander as A shoots might also drop the mantle around B or drop the screen in front of A. Doing this to a bystander would certainly involve using him to aid B. Of course, it may only be permissible to shoot the bullet at A who threatens B and not at a bystander, but that may just mean that it is permissible to use only A during his threatening act to aid his victim. The point is that we use A to produce some helpful effect for B other than stopping A's act while A presents a threat to B.

If we were able to stop A's action, we would clearly eliminate the threat to B. We might have to manipulate A in some way (for example, get him to make jerking movements) to interfere with his act, but this would still be our engaging in what has come to be referred to as "eliminative agency." By contrast, when we cannot stop A's action but see that some use of A can help us protect B from A's threat, possibly we will be engaging in what has come to be referred to as "opportunistic agency." (The following discussion should help explain why I say "possibly.")

The distinction between these two types of agency was drawn by Warren Quinn in trying to explain the Doctrine of Double Effect. He said (referring to the person we will harm as "victim" in cases to which abbreviations refer and whose details need not concern us):

One further bit of line-drawing remains....This difference may partly depend on whether the agent, in his strategy, sees the victim as an advantage or as a difficulty. In CC the doctor wants the fetus removed from the birth canal. Its presence there is a problem. In GP and TB, on the other hand, the availability of potential victims presents an opportunity. By bringing it about that certain things are true of them, the agents positively further their goals. Perhaps it would not be surprising if we regarded fatal or harmful exploitation as more difficult to justify than fatal or harmful elimination. If so, we might say that the doctrine strongly discriminates against direct agency that benefits from the presence of the victim (direct *opportunistic* agency) and more weakly discriminates against direct agency that aims to remove an obstacle or difficulty that the victim presents (direct *eliminative* agency).[59]

This quote suggests that whatever we do to someone who presents a difficulty in order to eliminate the difficulty involves eliminative agency, and it is only doing things to those who do not present a difficulty to eliminate a difficulty that involves opportunistic agency. On this understanding of the eliminative/opportunistic distinction, killing A to drop the screen or mantle would be eliminative, not opportunistic, agency (even though it manipulates A). Yet it seems to me that the way in which we eliminate the threat involves making use of opportunities and advantages that A presents quite independently of his presenting a threat, even though we act while he threatens. Hence, there may be combining (or blurring) of the two types of agency in our permissible intervention.

B. TORTURING TO BENEFIT

Suppose the arguments presented in Section II for the permissibility of torturing A (wide or narrow) to stop his act of attacking B were correct. Then if it is permissible to do what kills A in Killer Case (5) and its variants, it should be permissible to *torture* A (wide or narrow, in the manner described earlier) during his act to prevent the success of his attack and the harm from his attack, even if we cannot stop his act itself.[60]

Here is an example employing torture-narrow: In Killer Case (6), we deliberately cause A intense pain as he acts. We foresee that the pain will not be enough to get him to decide to refrain from attacking B in order to make the torture stop. However, we know that the pain will be enough, in combination with the strain involved in his act, to make him decide to move from where he stands to ease his pain. This will cause the protective mantle to fall around B. For reasons given above, this may involve using A to aid B (while it also prevents his harming him), and it may involve opportunistic as well as eliminative agency.

In sum, for any type of torture that physically could be done to someone held captive after he has committed an act that will kill a victim unless we do something, we can imagine a hypothetical case in which the same torture imposed while someone acts could stop the success of his attack or the harm from it. This is so, even if it does not stop the act itself. It seems likely that if it would be permissible to kill someone while he acts to stop his attack or the harm from it, it would be permissible to use some degree of torture, wide or narrow, while the person acts to stop the attack or harm from it, even if it cannot stop his act. The torture could substitute for killing him or be the only thing we can do to help B. Even if it were not permissible to kill him, some kinds of torture could still be proportional to stopping the attack or its harm. This shows that if it is not correct to restrict the notion of torture so that it applies only to what is done to someone after he acts while held captive, some torture could be morally permissible.[61] However, it does not show that doing the same thing to someone after he acts and while held captive is morally permissible.

IV. *Torture after Action*

A. EX POST IN GENERAL

Commonly, concerns about the possibility or morality of torture do not arise in connection with doing something to someone while he is acting in order to stop him from killing others, at least on the conception of an action that was employed in Sections II and III.[62] (Doing something to him while he is acting is likely to be thought of as an attempt to stop his act itself. In Section III, I tried to show that this need not be so.) Rather, concern focuses on torturing someone *after* he has done his act (e.g., set some device that *will* kill people). I shall call this "ex post torture."[63] The cases of ex post torture that are of most concern occur when the person to be tortured is currently under the control and in the custody of the proper authorities.[64] Ex post torture is, arguably, somewhat like the cases in Section III, because we do something to someone when we cannot stop his dangerous act. However, it is unlike those cases in that we do something to someone *after* he has acted (given a common conception of an action). (The cases in Section III are, therefore, a bridge between torturing someone to stop his act while he acts and torturing someone after he has acted in order to prevent harm from his act.) So let us imagine Killer Case (7), in which A has set a bomb that will shortly kill B unless we get the information from A about the location of the bomb and how to defuse it. Could it be permissible to torture A ex post (either wide or narrow) by causing him pain as in Killer Cases (1)–(4), if this were necessary and sufficient to save B from A's bomb?[65]

In order to deal with this question, it will help to imagine cases in which it might be useful to do harmful things other than torture (but also much less bad than death) to A ex post that would save B. For example, imagine Killer Case (8): A arranged for information about the bomb he set to be on a microchip implanted in his ear. To get the information and successfully save B, we would have to surgically operate on A's ear against his will, using proper medical procedures while A is under anesthesia. This would not involve torture, but it would violate his body and harm him by leaving him partially deaf. Those who object to ex post torture because it is done when someone is no longer actively threatening people should also object to such surgery undertaken to save B.

Suppose these same people think that, as a conceptual matter, torturing A (wide or narrow) can occur in (all or some of) Killer Cases (1)–(6). Suppose also that they think that in (some or all of) those cases, torture *and* also ear surgery could permissibly be done while A is in the process of doing his threatening acts, if they were (somehow) the least harmful ways to stop A's act, or even just the success of his attack or the harm from it (as in Section III). I think we can conclude from this set of views that these people, at least, are not concerned that *torture* per se is always impermissible. The issue for them is not torture but rather the possible moral difference between (i) physically or psychologically harming someone while he is attacking someone else in order to either directly interfere with or coercively stop his act, attack, or the harm from it, and (ii) physically or psychologically harming someone after he has acted to attack someone else, even though harming him would still stop the success of the attack or the harm to the victim.

Those who object to the ear surgery on A ex post would also object to killing A ex post to stop the attack on B, though this involved no torture. For example, if the microchip had been implanted in A's heart, and removing A's heart ex post is the only way to get the microchip, they would object. Even if objectors to ear surgery ex post thought that torturing was a distinctive wrong and were more reluctant to torture than to kill, they would not think that killing was permissible ex post when torture is not. Yet they would not object to killing A to stop his act of killing B or the harm from the act in earlier Killer Cases, if this were necessary.

It seems then that torture (wide or narrow) may be a "red herring" in the sense that at least the sort of torture employed in the Killer Cases seems permissible while an agent is actively attacking someone, and much that is not torture is standardly objected to if done to someone ex post. If torture were only permissible as a substitute for killing someone, as in Killer Cases (3) and (4), the fact that ex post killing is ruled out could explain why torture is not permissible ex post. However, I have suggested that some torture (and other lesser harms) would be permissible while an agent acts though they are not substitutes for killing and even when killing would be impermissible. Suppose this is true. Then if such torture and other harms less than death would be ruled out only ex post, it seems that it is "ex postness" that is the crucial issue: If one is opposed to ex post harm in general,[66] it is no wonder that one is opposed to ex post torture in particular. It is because we do not usually confront real-life cases in which torture applied during an act would stop an attacker's act, the success of his attack, or harm from it (directly or coercively), that the permissibility of torture and the separable issue of the permissibility of ex post harm have become confused.[67]

This does not mean that the distinction between torture and other harms is of no moral significance. If we have to decide whether to use one method or another when we have options, there may be things to be said against torture that cannot be said against other methods. However, if torture of the sort imagined in the Killer Cases is one's only option or the only alternative to some much greater harm, its distinctive features may not be what determines whether it is permissible. I have, of course, only been discussing cases that involve causing someone severe pain for an hour (in order to get him directly or coercively to stop his act, the success of his attack, or harm to his victim). It might be suggested that it is the severity of the torture, not whether it occurs during an act or ex post, that is crucial. It might be impermissible to severely torture someone (even rather than kill him) during his act as well as ex post.[68] Even though this is true, it will not explain why torture that would be permitted during an act should be thought to be impermissible ex post. In addition, in many cases where torture to stop an act would be impermissibly severe, killing would be permitted to stop the act. However, as noted, those who object to torture ex post would not permit doing what ex post kills in our cases either.

If ex postness is the real issue, then permitting some types of torture ex post would be a radical move not because of the use of torture per se but because it would open up the possibility that it is permissible to do many other things ex post to perpetrators that are usually thought to be impermissible in order to help their potential victims. Torture is often said to be contrary to our values. But it is more likely that it is ex post harm that is contrary to our values (with the exception of punishment).

Suppose we have correctly identified ex postness as the factor that *accounts* for opposition to many kinds of torture of captives. We still have to consider whether this factor *justifies* the opposition.

B. IS EX POSTNESS MORALLY SIGNIFICANT?

Let us now consider possible objections to and defenses of the moral significance of ex postness.

1. *Different Conception of Action.* The first objection concerns the very idea of "ex post an act." As noted above, Sussman thinks that someone who started a threat and refrains from giving information that could stop it is still engaged in *presenting* the threat. (This involves an alternative conception of an action.) On this account, that the wrongdoer is in custody and has finished setting a threatening device does not mean it is now ex post his act. (He also differs from someone who even wrongfully is not giving information to stop a threat but did not start the threat. Possibly, this other person is wrongfully maintaining the threat but he is not presenting it.)

Suppose Sussman's suggestion is correct and A is still engaged in presenting the threat in Killer Case (7). Then perhaps it would be as permissible to torture him (wide or narrow) as to torture A in Killer Cases (1)–(4) because we would be torturing while he is presenting a threat in order to stop his presenting it.[69] Indeed, if it were possible to stop A's refraining from giving information only by doing what will eventually kill him, Sussman might be committed to allowing this if he would permit A to be killed in Killer Cases (1)–(4). (How can aid from A be forthcoming, at least actively, if A is killed? Things done to A that will get him to actively give aid at t_1 could unavoidably cause his death at t_2. Of course, one could also imagine that killing A will result in some crucial information being revealed [as when the microchip is recovered from his heart in the variant on Killer Case (8) imagined above], independent of his actively providing it. However, I am not sure this would strictly count as stopping someone's refraining from aid, though it could stop his threat and the harm from it.)

2. *Harming versus Not Aiding.* However, suppose we are not sure Sussman is correct that A is presenting a threat to B when he refuses to stop the threat that he started.[70] It might still be possible to argue that having presented the threat, *ex post* refusing to stop it licenses the same treatment as presenting the threat would license. As this second objection to the moral significance of ex postness is not based on the view that A is still presenting a threat if he does not help stop it, it seems to raise the issue of the moral significance of A's harming versus A's not aiding. Indeed, this objection helps us see that the view that ex postness matters morally to what may be done to a wrongdoer may be based on the following argument: (1) Ex post, someone can only be failing to aid (sometimes by refraining from aid) rather than harming. (2) Failing to aid (even refraining from aid) is morally less significant than harming. (3) Hence, it is not permissible to do as much to someone to get him to aid ex post as it is to get him to not harm.[71] (Call this the Ex Post Argument.)

There are several concerns about this argument. First, in discussing Killer Case (5), we suggested that shooting A in order to drop a screen in front of his bullet (or a protective mantle around B) might constitute using A to aid B by protecting B from A's own threat. Suppose this description is correct and firing at A in Case (5) is permissible. Then ex post harm to a wrongdoer to stop the threat he started could not be impermissible just because it involves using the wrongdoer to aid his victim. Nor could it be wrong just because some ex post harm would be used coercively to get someone to act (or to elicit behavior) rather than just interfere with his act or the harm from it. For we considered cases in which it seemed permissible to cause A severe pain while he is releasing a threat at B in order to get A to do a different act or movement, even one that aids B in Killer Case (6), rather than the threatening one.

There is another point connected with the harming/not aiding distinction, but independent of the view that failing to aid is less significant than harming. It might be suggested that we may not impose harm ex post on a wrongdoer in order to aid his victim because doing so involves opportunistic agency. By contrast, it may be said, stopping the wrong-doer's harmful act would have involved eliminative agency, and this is favored relative to opportunistic agency.[72] However, in discussing Killer Case (5), we also suggested that firing a bullet at A in order to drop a screen or protective mantle might involve opportunistic agency in using A to stop his threat to B without stopping his act. Suppose this is correct and yet it is permissible to fire at A in Case (5). Then ex post harm to a wrongdoer to stop the threat he started could not be impermissible just because it involves opportunistic agency rather than eliminative agency. (Indeed, we could imagine that what is to be done to A ex post is necessary to drop a screen or protective mantle so that B is not harmed. It is hard to see how this could involve opportunistic agency to aid B, yet what is done in Case [5] does not.)

Suppose ex post harm is not unique in eliciting aid rather than just stopping harmful acts, and in involving opportunistic rather than eliminative agency, yet harm during an act that has these characteristics can be permissible. Then if ex post harm is impermissible, we will not be able to explain the significance of ex postness itself in terms of the harming/not aiding distinction or the opportunistic/eliminative distinction.

Yet another concern about the Ex Post Argument applies even if Killer Case (5) does not involve permissible instances of opportunistic agency to make a wrongdoer aid his victim. For the nonconsequentialist view that someone may be required to suffer greater losses in order not to harm than to aid usually contrasts those who would harm with non-aiders who have not already threatened the person they would aid. Hence, it is consistent with a moral distinction between harming and not aiding that those who have presented a threat of harm are required to suffer, or may have imposed on them, as much to aid their potential victim as to stop the act that would harm someone. However, it may be worth distinguishing what a person who has presented a threat must do or may have imposed on him to help *stop his threat*, and what he must do to aid his victim in other ways. This distinction could be relevant even when it is clear that the person is still presenting a threat. For example, suppose someone is driving a car that is about to crash into people although the driver is not trying to kill anyone. (Call this the Morally Innocent Driver Case.) The innocent driver might be shot at or be required to sacrifice his life to swerve the threatening device for which he is responsible. Suppose that he is unable to swerve but can save his victim by jumping out and, at the cost of his own life, pulling the victim away from the car. Perhaps he is not morally required to save his victim in this way.[73] Even if this distinction were important when it is a wrongdoer, not the innocent driver, who must aid, in Killer Cases (7) and (8) the costs that would be imposed on A *are* for aid in stopping his threatening device.

And yet, we could imagine that the innocent driver of the threatening car is thrown from it as it heads towards his victims. He is no longer driving towards his victims, but his car could be stopped by our harming him as he sits on the sideline. (Call this the Sideline Case.) Are the costs that could now permissibly be imposed on him to stop the car the same as the costs we could impose or require when he is driving the car? Intuitively, they are not. This supports the significance of ex postness (whether or not it depends on the harming/not aiding distinction and/or the eliminative/opportunistic distinction). So the Sideline Case suggests that sometimes it could be permissible to impose certain costs on someone to stop his threatening device while he threatens with it, although not once he does not threaten with it. (This is so even though it continues to be a threat.)

However, the driver on the sideline should, presumably, do something easy that he alone can do to stop his car—for example, press a button. Suppose he refrains from doing what he should do. May we then impose the easy cost on him (e.g., painlessly move his finger to the button that requires his fingerprint to operate)? May we impose greater costs on him to get him to press the button if this were necessary, even if not as great as when he was driving the car? These seem to me to be important questions. One question deals with how much he owes ex post by comparison to during an act. The other question deals with what cost we may impose on him so that the threat is stopped.[74]

These questions bear on cases of deliberate harm, for someone might try to justify torture in Killer Case (7) to get A to stop the threat he deliberately started on the grounds that he is deliberately refraining from easy aid (e.g., all he must do is give information). Even if giving the aid is not easy, it is something he should do that he is not doing.[75] But can deliberately starting the threat and wrongfully failing to provide aid he should be giving justify making him give it? For example, if all A had to do was press a button to stop his threat but he refused, would it be permissible to painlessly move his finger on the button? If so, this would involve manipulative opportunistic agency in order to provide aid. I find it hard to believe we should not do this to A. And may we impose greater costs than could have initially been required of him ex post—even if the costs are not as great as may permissibly be imposed during an act—that will elicit or prompt the provision of the aid originally required (i.e., pressing the button)? If so, this might justify some torture ex post.

Now suppose that the only way A could aid ex post at all was by doing something that involved as great a cost to him as the torture we would have to impose to elicit easy aid from him in the previous example. If he refrained from aiding at such a larger cost, would he also be failing to do what he should to stop his threat? Presumably, more than this cost would have been required from him, or could have been imposed on him, to stop his threat while he was actively bringing it about (even in order to bring down the screen or mantle in Killer Case [5]). To think that a wrongdoer owes this much ex post, even if not as much as could have been demanded or imposed during his threatening activity, amounts to reducing to a great degree the moral significance of ex postness with respect to amount of aid owed, at least in the case of deliberate wrongdoers. By contrast, to focus on how *little* it would cost a wrongdoer to aid ex post, as justification for torturing in Killer Case (7) when he fails to aid, suggests that even in the case of wrongdoers, ex postness has a significant role in determining what *initially* can be required of him to stop his threat. However, if his refraining from easy aid could justify imposing torture in Killer Case (7), this would show that the importance of ex postness in determining what he owes is compatible with the permissibility of some torture in eliciting as much as he owes.

Nevertheless, it might seem odd that we could be licensed to impose a greater cost on A ex post, because he wrongfully refuses to give easy aid, than what he owes ex post just because he wrongfully released a threat to B. What might make sense of this is the permissibility of responding with greater costs to what the agent wrongfully does when he is actually doing it; ex post to starting a threat, he is refusing aid he owes; he is not starting the threat then. And yet, his having started the threat would be relevant to the permissibility of our imposing the additional cost to get him to give aid that he owes when he refrains. For it would not be permissible to impose as high an additional cost to get someone to fulfill a duty to aid from which he refrains when he was not involved in starting the threat.

We should now consider whether refraining from aid one should have given is necessary for the permissibility of imposing some ex post torture to get a wrongdoer to aid his victim. Consider Killer Case (9): A is morally responsible for having pushed a boulder onto B, who will be crushed unless A helps remove the boulder which he is still near. There is no way that A could move the boulder, as he collapsed unconscious after his attack, so he is not refraining from giving aid. Presumably, we could still permissibly impose on A some small cost that he owes B in aid, if this were necessary to save B. (For example, from a distance, we could permissibly move his body so that it pushes the boulder off B's body at the cost of a few scratches to him.) But what if much more would have to be done to unconscious A? For example, suppose that only if we shock him for an hour from a distance in a controlling and gradated fashion, causing him intense pain, will his body be thrust onto the boulder, moving it away from B. This way of saving B would involve wide-torturing A, I believe. Could it be permissible to do this to A in order to save B, if we could permissibly have done it to him when he was pushing the boulder onto B, in order to stop his act or the harm from it? In this case, we are not getting A to give aid that he refuses to give on his own.[76]

It is harder (perhaps impossible) to construct a narrow-torture variant on Killer Case (9). This is because narrow-torture would involve making the wrongdoer decide to give in and help his victim. But this implies that he was refraining from simply helping.[77] However, we might try to show that it is not A's refraining that justifies either getting him to costlessly push the boulder or our narrow-torture of him by constructing a case in which he refrains, but not wrongfully, from aiding his victim. For example, suppose that members of the organization to which A belongs will kill his innocent family members if he aids, unless he is being tortured to do so. Even though we might then think he was not wrong to refrain from aiding his victim, his responsibility for starting the threat might be said to be sufficient grounds to narrow-torture him (in the manner described) in order to get him to save his victim.[78]

By contrast, suppose that C, who had no part in threatening B, *is* refusing easy aid to B because he intends B's death. Suppose we have a choice of torturing either A after he collapsed or C (in the way described), in order to accomplish the rescue of B. Those who would minimize the significance of ex postness in the case of a wrongdoer would say that if we may torture anyone, it is A and not C, even when A is in a state of collapse and never refrained from aiding. A's being morally responsible for the wrong of pushing a boulder onto B could make A morally liable to being tortured to rescue B, but the wrong of failing to rescue B alone does not make C liable to similar treatment.[79]

In Killer Case (9) and its variant, on any view of an action, we would not be torturing A while he is presenting a threat to B, but *after* this is over (ex post). If doing this were permissible in order to stop A's threat to B, it would not be the combination of being morally responsible for wrongfully starting the threat *and* wrongfully refraining from stopping it that is needed to make A a target for being harmed in order to help B. Rather, someone's being morally responsible for wrongfully starting the threat would have a dominant role in making him liable to some types of costs in order to aid his victim. Hence, this liability would be independent of whether his not stopping the threat constitutes his continuing to present the threat or a wrongful failure to stop his threat. His ex post liability might arise because A has a special obligation to B to stop the threat to him, in virtue of his being morally responsible for the wrong of having pushed a boulder on B *and* when he himself cannot fulfill his obligation, we should see to it that the costs he owes are extracted to stop his threat. (This could be true when he is to be tortured [in the manner described] only if he owes more than easy aid.) Or it might be that independent of whether he owes it to his victim to undergo some costs to aid and we are extracting his debt, he is liable to our imposing this cost on him, given the wrong he has done in starting the threat.[80]

Similarly, in cases where torture-narrow would be necessary to get from a terrorist information that would stop the imminent threat he started to many people, one usually thinks the terrorist could provide the information if he wanted to. This might lead some to think he is still presenting the threat or, at least, *doing* something else wrong in addition to having started a threat. But we can imagine wide- and narrow-torture cases where this is not so. Consider Killer Case (10): A terrorist suffers amnesia directly after setting a bomb that is about to go off. (We can imagine that he threatens one person or many.) He is still near his bomb's site and could defuse the bomb by decoding it, if he remembered the code. Only gradated, painful electric shocks that we can administer at a distance over an hour can break through the amnesia. (This is torture-wide.) Once this happens, continuing torture can lead him to decide to defuse the bomb as a way to end the torture. (This is torture-narrow.) When the terrorist is originally not refraining from aid, how can it be said he is still presenting the threat or wrongfully not aiding? Could it be said, however, that the terrorist is guilty of maintaining and presenting the threat if he refuses to allow torture to relieve his amnesia (supposing he knows we could reverse it)?[81] Then imagine that he collapses mentally after setting his bomb and is not capable of deciding about anything. Only torture-wide (in the manner described) would bring him out of this mental collapse so that he remembers the code. If continual pain is administered to get him to give in and defuse the bomb once he is able to recall the code but he refrains in order to save his family from reprisals, we are dealing with torture-narrow. *If* it were permissible to torture in Killer Case (9) and its variant, then given what has been said in previous parts of this chapter, it would be puzzling if it were impermissible to torture the terrorist in Killer Case (10) too.

3. *Implications*. This brings us back to where Shue started. Namely, may we harm people even when it is clear that they are not currently presenting a threat (as in the case when A collapses after pushing the

boulder onto B) in order to stop the threat to their victims? It may seem puzzling that the reasons that make it permissible to do something to a person to stop his harmful act should not also make it permissible to do even the same thing to him (a) to stop his successfully attacking his victim and (b) to stop his victim from being harmed by his attack, whether we do this (c) while he acts (without, however, stopping his act) or (d) after he acts. And yet, at least in cases where an agent was not deliberately trying to harm his victim (as in our Sideline Case), ex postness seems to make a big moral difference. Nevertheless, contrary to Shue, it may be that ex postness should have less significance when a wrongdoer deliberately tried to harm his victim, both in deciding what he owes and what may be imposed.

If we kill or torture an agent who is about to kill someone (as in Killer Cases [1]–[4]), we are doing something to him to help his targeted victim, but we are also either directly interfering with a wrong act or getting him to stop his act when he is performing it. Hence, we are responding to him as an agent at the time of his agency and not harming him on account of his past agency. The desire to be able to say that one is responding to someone as an agent at the time of his agency and also, perhaps, stopping him from acting (directly or by getting him to act differently) as opposed to only stopping his attack's success or its harm (as in Killer Case [5]) may lie behind Sussman's focus on cases where the terrorist actively refrains from giving information. If we torture A in Killer Case (7) as he refrains from aid, Sussman might say that we would then be trying to stop an agent's presenting a threat at the time he presents it or, at the very least, stop his actively refraining from aid. But if it were permissible to torture A in Killer Case (9) when he is not refraining from aid, then we would just make use of him after his act to stop his threat on account of his past agency. We are being asked to take seriously that this might be permissible.

Above, I noted that Sussman's view that a wrongdoer who started a bomb is still presenting a threat when he refuses to stop it could imply that it is permissible to do what will *kill* the wrongdoer if only this will stop his refraining. Suppose that moral responsibility for wrongfully creating the threat, with or without refraining from aid, might make one liable to some kinds of torture (or other harm) to stop the threat in

Killer Cases (9) and (10). Then some might claim that these factors also make one liable to being killed ex post to stop one's threat. They would be denying that there is a middle ground that allows some, but not complete, similarity between what may be done ex post and during the presentation of a threat.

If any argument that implied the permissibility of some torture ex post also implied the permissibility of killing ex post, this could be seen as a reductio of the argument for some ex post torture. Still, rejecting both killing and torture ex post would reinforce the point that the problem is not with torture in particular but with ex post harm in general. This is consistent with some torture and killing being permissible sometimes (for example, to stop an unjust killing) while the wrongdoer is actively presenting the threat. Suppose we reject the moral permissibility of killing the wrongdoer ex post if this were necessary and sufficient to stop his threat but accept the moral permissibility of some lesser harms, including some torture ex post. We would then have to do more work to show why ex postness has enough moral significance to exclude killing but not some other types of harm.

C. UNCERTAINTY

To conclude this discussion of Killer Cases (7)–(10), recall that I argued that torturing A could be permissible in Killer Cases (1)–(4), even when we have some doubts that A is trying to kill B, will succeed in doing so, and we can succeed in saving B by torturing A. This conclusion may apply to an argument for torture ex post. That is, suppose that in the absence of these doubts, it was sometimes permissible to torture ex post (or if refraining from aid involved continued presentation of a threat). Then it may also be permissible to torture a wrongdoer if this is necessary to stop the threat to his victim(s), even if we have some doubts that he was (or still is) trying to kill them, that he will have done (or is doing) something that will succeed in killing them, and that what we do to him will save them. This seems to be true, at least when the combination of uncertainties is far below the level that should cause us to refrain from torturing A in Killer Cases (1)–(4).[82]

D. THE POSSIBLE ROLE OF CUSTODY

Notice that I constructed Killer Cases (9) and (10) so that the perpetrator is (i) *still outside our custody* and (ii) *he must himself be involved in the removal of the threat to his victim.* I did this in order to focus on the possible moral significance of ex postness (and whatever might make it significant), whether it occurs when someone is in custody or not in custody. In the cases that Shue and Sussman discuss and in most realistic cases, a wrongdoer *is* in our custody and *we* would have to act on information he gives. (Being in our custody is not merely being subject to our control because, for example, the terrorist on-site in Killer Case [10], as I described it, is also subject to our control but not in our custody.) We shall now merely raise the questions whether the wrongdoer being our captive and the wrongdoer not directly aiding are morally significant factors on their own or in conjunction with ex postness.

It is possible to imagine that a captive in our custody is the only one able to directly defuse a bomb he started. (That is, we cannot merely act on his information.) I do not think that the fact that he alone could defuse it, a characteristic that he would then share with the terrorist in Case (10), could play an important role in distinguishing him morally from a captive who must only provide information on which we can act. Hence, the fact that the on-site terrorist has to defuse the bomb himself does not affect whether torturing him is permissible.

This leaves the possibility that someone's being in our custody or our having placed him in our custody may make a moral difference to what it is permissible to do to him ex post in order to stop (directly or coercively) the threat he started. If a terrorist were to begin an attack while in our custody, I do not think there would be greater moral restrictions on what could be done to stop his actively presenting the threat than if he were not in our custody. Perhaps those who have custody have a special responsibility for their captives that limits what they may do only ex post. It is not clear why, but if this were so, then it could be neither torture (wide or narrow) nor harm being ex post, nor a combination of these, that would suffice to make ex post torture of our *captive* impermissible. It might take the fact that someone is in our custody to make ex post torture or other ex post harm morally impermissible for the sake of stopping the threat the wrong-doer started. We would need to investigate the possibility that this factor could override any permission to ex post torture wrongdoers who are not our captives for the sake of stopping their threats. (If being in our custody had this effect, we might face a choice between capturing a wrongdoer to prevent his creating new threats and leaving him free in order to stop the threats he has already started.)

V. *Some Others' Views*

A. THRESHOLD DEONTOLOGY

In his article, Sussman leaves open the question of whether it is ever ultimately permissible to torture-narrow people, even if he believes that there is a special type of reason against torture-narrow. Shue also does not argue that torture is absolutely morally impermissible. Some moral philosophers support threshold deontology, where this means that when the overall bad consequences of not transgressing someone's right is great enough, the right is overridden. (An alternative way of understanding the matter is that the right when properly specified does not apply in certain circumstances.) So, for example, some may think that a right not to be tortured (and a duty not to torture) will get overridden (or specified away) when many innocent lives are at stake. It is important to distinguish the arguments I have been considering from this one.

One reason is that the threshold argument may apply as well to torturing an *innocent bystander*, if a great many people would perish unless he were tortured. An argument that showed doing this to be permissible would have to be very different from the argument(s) that I have been considering, which point to what may be done to an agent who created a threat for the sake of his potential victims.

As was pointed out above, and exemplified in the Killer Cases, the arguments I have been considering do not require that there be many lives at stake in order for some torture to be justified. The fact that some who seek to justify torture often raise "ticking bomb" cases involving thousands of people suggests that they are not just considering whether it is justified to torture a known terrorist in order to prevent harm to his own victim(s), as I have been doing. Rather, they may be trying to justify torturing someone whom they only suspect of knowing about terrorism, in order to help people who have been or will be threatened by others. Torturing such people may be unjustifiable, according to threshold deontologists, unless the lives of thousands or more are at stake.[83]

Hence, even if the part of my argument that investigates the permissibility of ex post harm may seem to consider radical options, the fact that my argument is limited to investigating the relation between an agent and his victim makes it, in one way, conservative.

B. AGENT-FOCUSED OBJECTIONS

Throughout this chapter, I have been concerned with what I take to be the most important objection to the permissibility of torture, namely, what it would do to the person tortured. Some offer another objection to the permissibility of torture, namely, what it would do to the agent who tortures. One version of this concern is that the agent who tortures would thereby betray his values if he is, in general, opposed to treating people in this way.[84] This is hardly a strong objection, for it does nothing to explain why an agent should have these values. If he has them because torture is inconsistent with the status of the victim, then the objection is at base victim-, not agent-focused. The victim-focused objection is what I have been examining.

Another version of the agent-focused objection claims that the agent is corrupted by the process of torturing someone, and he should avoid being corrupted. This version of the agent-focused objection, by contrast to the first, tries to justify an agent having values that rule out torture on the grounds of his avoiding corruption. However, it at least *seems* that torturing someone could be corrupting, only if torturing is wrong on other grounds. That is, the prospect of corruption *seems to presuppose* that what will be done is wrong, rather than providing a reason to believe it is wrong.

If so, we would need another explanation for why torturing is wrong, on the whole or in part, besides its leading to corruption of the torturer. Suppose we had an account of why torture is wrong. Then it seems misguided to think that the strongest objection to the wrong act is not what makes it wrong but that it makes an agent who does it into a wrong-doer. It is especially misguided to think that agents themselves should avoid wrong acts because of the effect on themselves. Rather they should avoid wrong acts because of the properties that make the act wrong.

Finally, it might be said, there is a way to be corrupted by torturing independently of its being wrong to torture for victim-focused reasons. This way is to use the occasion of torturing as an opportunity to indulge feelings of dominance or sadism. However, not all persons who torture need have these feelings. And in order to ensure that an agent is not corrupted in this way, he could even start a pain- or fear-causing machine, after which he only monitors the event. Using such machinery would reduce the risk of indulging bad feelings. If torture were still wrong, this would show that this agent-focused argument against torture is not crucial.

VI. *Conclusion*

Table 1 summarizes some factors I have emphasized in my discussion. I will not fill in the answers to how these factors interact, so that the table merely emphasizes that these are questions one must deal with regardless of how one fills in the boxes.

My conclusions are that during his wrongful act, torturing someone in some ways would be permissible to stop the act or harm from it. This includes torture-narrow, in which we do not incapacitate the agent or elicit an automatic response, but instead use means such as intense pain to get him to decide not to do his harmful act or to do another act. We might also elicit the communication of information that stops his act. If we cannot stop his act by these means, I suggested that they may be used on him during his act to stop the success of his attack or the harm from it, even though this might involve using opportunistic agency to get a wrongdoer to do an act to aid his victim. If these conclusions are correct, then some torture is morally permissible.

I then argued that if some torture is permissible during an act and much harm that is not torture is thought to be impermissible ex post an act, it may be that with respect to some kinds of torture, it is the ex post-ness of torture rather than torture *per se* that is objectionable. What may

Table 1:

		Harm		
		Torture		Nontorture
		Wide	Narrow	

During Act
(1) as substitute
(2) on own
	(a) To stop harmful act
	    and/or
	(b) To stop success of
	    attack and harm
	    from it			

Ex Post	(a) In custody and
	    refraining from
	    owed aid
	(b) In custody and not
	    refraining from
	    owed aid
	(c) Not in custody and
	    refraining from
	    owed aid
	(d) Not in custody and
	    not refraining from
	    owed aid			

sometimes be crucial is not what torture is but when it is done. I investigated and raised doubts about whether ex post torture might be morally objectionable because of a moral distinction between harming and not aiding, or between eliminative and opportunistic agency. I suggested that if arguments that justify some torture during an act could be extended to justify some ex post torture, this conclusion would be radical not because it permits torture per se but because it would permit sometimes doing harm in general to wrongdoers ex post to stop their threats.

Finally, I considered the possibility that even if ex postness did not always rule out some torture of a wrongdoer to stop his threat, his being in custody might. If so, then neither torture per se nor it in combination with ex postness would always be sufficient to explain the impermissibility of ex post torture of wrongdoers necessary to stop lethal threats previously started by those wrongdoers now in custody.[85]

Notes

1. F. M. Kamm, *Intricate Ethics: Rights, Responsibilities, and Permissible Harm* (New York: Oxford University Press, 2007), p. 238.
2. See Henry Shue, "Torture," *Philosophy & Public Affairs* 7 (Winter 1978): 124–43.
3. See David Sussman, "What's Wrong with Torture?," *Philosophy & Public Affairs* 33 (Winter 2004): 1–33. Published online December 16, 2004, www3. interscience.wiley.com.
4. The fact that one would torture only known terrorists does not mean one would be torturing them to stop their own terrorist plots. The latter is an additional assumption in my discussion.
5. Suppose it were permissible to kill one innocent person to save ten others from being killed. Then it would be no more true of them than of the innocent person who was killed to save them that they had a status that made it impermissible to kill them to save others from being killed. By contrast, if it is impermissible to kill one, and we do not kill him, it remains true of the ten that it is impermissible to kill them for similar purposes—their status is retained—even if what happens is that they are killed. For my discussion of these issues, see my *Morality, Mortality, Vol. 2* (New York: Oxford University Press, 1996), among other places.
6. By "could be morally permissible in some cases," I do not mean to suggest that sometimes it may be morally permissible to torture when it is against the law to do so. Hence, to investigate whether torture could ever be morally permissible is analogous to having investigated, at a time when abortion was still illegal, whether abortion could ever be morally permissible. (An objection to investigating the morality of what is currently an illegal practice was raised by Jeremy Waldron.) It remains true, however, that it could sometimes even be morally permissible to violate the law.
7. See, for example, his disclaimer in "Torture," n. 15, p. 138, and his remarks in n. 11, p. 133.
8. As opposed to harming them as side effects.
9. Thomas Christiano suggested that being in a position to control and gradate the pain over a period of time, rather than merely doing something that causes pain to someone (such as pouring acid on them) might be important in order to distinguish torturing a threat from doing other things to stop him.
10. Shue, "Torture," pp. 130–1.

11. However, the limits exist because of normative, not physical, considerations. So the sense of "possible" Shue is interested in is really normatively possible. I shall consider this issue in greater detail below.

12. Sussman points this out, too, in "What's Wrong with Torture," pp. 17–18.

13. Ibid., pp. 5–8.

14. Ibid., p. 8.

15. Personal communication from Sussman.

16. When pain is not caused, and not believed to be caused, by another person, someone can still experience a conflict between identifying with his body's plea to stop the pain and a desire to resist doing something that might stop the pain. Insofar as he instinctively assents to his body's plea to stop the pain but also resists doing what would stop it, his agency is divided against itself. This part of the phenomenon that Sussman describes is quite common and not limited to torture. But Sussman says (in his comments on an earlier version of this chapter) that he is concerned with a particular form of such division, in which one experiences some part of one's agency as also in a way "not-me," but as of someone else in particular (the torturer).

17. This was emphasized to me by Arthur Ripstein. The distinction between coercion and interference seems to be extremely important to Kantians. It will help to understand this to consider how Barbara Herman has discussed this issue in connection with two forms of Kant's Categorical Imperative test for the permissibility of maxims of conduct.

    In her "Murder and Mayhem" (reprinted in Barbara Herman, *The Practice of Moral Judgment* [Cambridge, MA: Harvard University Press, 1993], pp. 113–31), Herman says,

    > Although many violent acts are coercive (and so pose no special problem for the CC (Contradiction in Conception) test if coercion is rejected by it), it will not do to claim that killing is a limiting case of coercion. A coercive act aims at the control of a person's will; killing does not (at least not of the will of the person killed). In killing, someone is prevented from doing anything at all, but he is not made to do something against his will. There is a significant difference between threatening pain or twisting your arm (or even threatening to kill) to keep you from joining the opposition party and killing you to achieve the same result.... Killing (and noncoercive violence in general) poses a moral problem that needs to be kept separate from that of coercion. (p. 119)

She goes on to say that

> general features of willing contain the points at which the will is sub-
> ject to possible manipulation and interference, where agents' actions
> may be brought under the control of another. Beliefs can be manipu-
> lated, desires can be altered, induced, enhanced, and so on. This is the
> arena of the CC test. The conditions of agency that enter CW
> (Contradiction in Will) arguments are not characteristics of willing as
> such. They are the features that characterize the limits of our powers
> as agents: we are both physically vulnerable and mortal....
>
> Here is where one might draw the line between violence and coer-
> cion. [C]oercion involves a more direct attack on agency than does
> any act of (mere) violence. Its intent is to subvert and control the will
> of another.... in willing maxims of deceit and coercion to be universal
> laws,... we in effect give over our agency to the agency of others (we
> become but one of many who determine what we will). A universal
> law involving the dispersal of agency cannot be conceived as a law for
> rational agents.
>
> Unlike coercion or deception, which involves assault on the integ-
> rity of willing itself, the object of violent action is not the will but a
> person's body. (Threats of violence and threats involving violence are
> other matters.) Coercion involves an attack on agency; violence, an
> attack on its conditions. Although violent actions usually prevent an
> agent from doing what he wills, they do not (they cannot) control
> willing....
>
> The CI [categorical imperative] procedure would seem to sort
> morally wrong "natural" actions into two kinds: (1) impingements
> on the constitutive elements of willed action (threats and coercion
> manipulate desires; deceit manipulates the circumstances of delib-
> eration), and (2) discounting the conditions of agency (vio-
> lence, indifference to self-development, or the true needs of others.
> (pp. 125–6)

She notes that it may be surprising that the duty not to intentionally kill is
derived by the CW test in the way imperfect duties are, while duties against
coercion derive from the CC Test and are perfect duties. (This raises the
question of whether her views imply that one of these types of assaults on
rational agency can be justified by factors that cannot justify the other.)
While both Sussman and Herman emphasize the difference between

coercive and obstructive interference, Sussman wants to emphasize that in torture coercion comes about through violent action on the body (whereas Herman emphasizes the obstructive rather than coercive uses of violence).

18. Kristi Olson raised this point.

19. He said this in comments on an earlier version of this chapter.

20. However, certain judgments expressed by Sussman (to be discussed below) seem inconsistent with this conclusion. Nevertheless, even if the conclusion is correct, this does not mean that no cases of self- or other-defense could involve torture on Sussman's account. I have already pointed out that he seems to think these are possible. See pp. 10–11.

21. The distinction between torture-narrow and -wide is not the same as the (supposed) distinction between torture and "torture-lite." Torture-wide could be "lite" because little pain is used to incapacitate someone or nonlite because much pain causing permanent damage is used, and torture-narrow could be nonlite because much pain causing permanent damage is used to motivate someone's action or lite because little pain is used.

22. There are other problems with requiring that torture involve having total physical power over one's captives (rather than seemingly total moral or legal authority over them). For example, suppose someone is physically unable to do something that causes only minor discomfort to someone, but he can do things that cause major discomfort. It would be bizarre to claim that he is not torturing when he does the latter just because he lacks total power. Yet, it was complained (by Tanina Rostain) that in considering hypothetical cases in which an agent can only affect someone at a distance in one very painful way in order to get him to do something, I was failing to capture the essence of torture, namely that there is a context of total control. There may certainly be something objectionable with having total control (physical, moral, and legal) of someone. However, I suggest, such power is not only not a necessary condition for torture, but it is not the most objectionable part of an event that includes torture. This is shown by our hypothetical case: What is done to the victim would not be worse if it were done when the torturer had the capacity to also cause minor discomfort. In addition, suppose that someone has total power but never uses it to do anything distressing to his captive. When the captive is released, does he have as great a complaint as a person to whom something very distressing was done by an agent who did not have the same total power? I think not.

23. Some objections to torture focus on what it does to the torturer. I think these are weaker objections and shall consider them at the end of the chapter.

24. Even Kantians, such as Herman and Sussman, can agree to this. Consider how Herman argues in "Murder and Mayhem" that some intentional killings can be justified after she has argued that they are ordinarily ruled out by the CW (Contradiction in Will) test, while coercion is ruled out by the CC (Contradiction in Conception) test. (See n. 17, above, on this.) She says:

> In rejecting the general maxim of violence, the CW argument...shows that acts that use or harm the human body may not be regarded simply as available means for our various purposes....It establishes a moral presumption against violence...putting the burden of argument on the agent who would be violent to explain why what he would do is not governed by the terms of the presumption....
>
> Let us take self-defense as the test case...It is not that I may kill in order to keep myself from becoming dead—something I do not want to happen....What a maxim of aggression or violence involves, morally speaking, is the discounting of my agency. The aggressor would use me (take my life) for his purposes. This is what I resist and claim moral title to refuse....it is not the fact of death but the death as a means to the aggressor's purposes that gives moral title to resistance and self-defense. The circumstances of aggression rebut the presumption against violence.
>
> This same fact blocks reciprocity of complaint....I am not acting to save my life as such, but to resist the use of my agency (self) by another....Thus, since my maxim of resistance is not a maxim of aggression as a means, the original aggressor cannot renew his attack on morally superior grounds....
>
> The justification of self-defense does not devalue the aggressor because he is guilty of aggression. He forfeits no moral title;...the fact of his undiminished agency and value grounds a proportionality of response...because, in limiting my action where possible, I demonstrate the moral regard he is still owed....The action of resistance needs to be guided by what is necessary to defuse the actual or perceived threat, constrained by other regulative maxims and concerns. If violence in self-defense is justified as an act of resistance to aggression, it would seem to be justified as an act of last resort....

> Since the justification for resistance is not that I may act to save my life, but to resist the misuse of my life or body as the life or body of a rational agent, it is not clear what difference it makes if the self I protect is not mine. (pp. 128–31)

I have several questions about Herman's view, as I understand it. It seems to me that killing an aggressor in self- or other defense can be permissible when an aggressor would impose (1) large bodily harm, not just death, on someone (2) against that person's will. Because Herman sees the loss of one's life as an attack on the conditions of one's agency (see n. 17 above), she might seem to be focusing on how the loss of one's life will make it impossible to be an agent in the future. However, when she focuses on resisting an aggressor's attempt to use one for his purposes, she focuses on how the attack is contrary to what someone has now willed, that is, that his body should not be used. This focus is, in part, correct, I think. However, this attack contrary to someone's current will is not a direct attack on current agency, since there is no manipulation of the person's desires or intentions per se, as would occur if someone coercively got us to agree to let our body be attacked now. Furthermore, the harm against which one may be defended by killing an attacker need not be of a type that would undermine the conditions of one's agency. So an aggressor could be killed if he tries to cut off one's arm quickly and painlessly, even if lacking an arm would not undermine one's rational agency. Finally, it is neither sufficient nor necessary to justify killing that an aggressor "discounts" my agency. First, an aggressor who disrespects one's current decision not to be kicked may not be killed because the harm one would suffer is not great enough. Second, it may be permissible to kill someone who will severely harm someone else only as a side effect, with no intention to make use of "death as a means to the aggressor's purposes."

In sum, I think that concern with agency should focus on disrespecting an agent's current decision and not downplay the significance of large losses that an agent decides not to suffer that have nothing to do with his losing his agency if he suffers them.

Although Herman discusses how the presumption against violence may be overcome in "Murder and Mayhem," she does not discuss whether and when the presumption against coercive violence (such as torture-narrow) may be overridden in dealing with an aggressor who aims to kill someone, whether he does or does not have coercive purposes.

25. This is the other case discussed in the initial quote from *Intricate Ethics*.

26. This need not imply that we are permitted or required to use means that effectively stop A's act and that are least bad for A. For example, if we could stop him from killing B by sending him to Club Med (even at no cost to ourselves), we need not do the latter rather than impose a small injury on him. (I owe this point to a student at the University of Arizona.) In addition, I emphasize that I am arguing that it may be important to what we should do, that torture is less bad for A than death is for A. This is not the same as arguing that we should do something because it would be less bad for A than what A would otherwise do to B. For given that A is attacking B, I believe it is not out of proportion to do worse things to A in order to stop him than he would do to B. For example, if A would only torture B for several hours or paralyze his legs permanently, it would still be permissible to kill A to stop him.

27. On what makes death bad, see Thomas Nagel's "Death," reprinted in his *Mortal Questions* (New York: Cambridge University Press, 1996), and my *Morality, Mortality, Vol. 1* (New York: Oxford University Press, 1993), chs. 1–3.

28. See my *Morality, Mortality, Vol. 1*.

29. David McCarthy, in comments on a shorter version of this chapter, suggested that I was relying on an intrapersonal consequentialist view in claiming that it is better for B to be tortured than to be killed. I think he is wrong. My emphasis on the narrative structure of a life, in *Morality, Mortality* Vol. 1, also supports this.

30. This was suggested to me by David Luban (in conversation).

31. Suppose causing A an hour of intense pain even when he does not believe it will end in an hour is better for him than being killed. It might then be asked, is torturing him rather than killing him not like a painful medical treatment undertaken to keep a patient alive? And if we would not say the medical treatment was torture, why should we say A is being tortured in Killer Case (3)? My response to this is in three parts: (1) In most cases when medical treatment is painful or humiliating, it is as a side effect, not as an intended means to the patient's greater good. By contrast, in Killer Case (3), the suffering that is the lesser evil for A relative to his death is an intended means to the goal of preventing *B's* death. However, we can imagine medical cases in which the suffering is an intended means to the patient's greater good. For example, suppose that the only way to stop a patient from falling into a permanent coma is to keep him in intense pain, because only intense pain will get him to try to resist us, and it is this act of resistance that we try

to bring forth in order to prevent the coma. In this case, would it be wrong to say that we are torturing the patient, but for his own good? Even if it were wrong to say this, there are other factors to consider. (2) In medical cases, we are trying to save the patient from an evil that we ourselves would not otherwise impose on him. Rather, the evil is a bodily dysfunction that we seek to eliminate and have no use for. In Killer Case (3), by contrast, we *would* impose the greater evil of death to which torture is the alternative in order to save B. Imposing suffering on A in order to prevent A's death, when we have it in our power to more directly prevent his death (by not killing him) is an additional contrast with painful medical care. This contrast helps make clear that when we intentionally cause the pain to the patient, we do so because it helps to stop the greater evil of his coma. By contrast, we do not need to torture someone to stop the greater evil of our killing him; we could just not kill him. Rather, we need to torture him in order to save B. (Here is a better analogy to the medical case where we would not impose the greater evil: M will kill N to get his money unless we torture N to get his money to M. In this case, we could correctly think of ourselves as acting solely out of concern for N if we prevent his death, and yet be very clear that we would be torturing him to get money to M.) (3) Finally, consider those who are tortured in prisons around the world in order to dissuade them from further political activities. Should we really withdraw this label if we find out that their being tortured by their state was the alternative to their being killed by the state?

32. Sussman distinguishes both interrogational torture and ordeals from masochistic practices to which someone might consent because the practice has a purpose that the person could reasonably share. Sussman seems to think that its being reasonable to consent makes the practices not be torture at all. But one might have thought that the fact that someone could reasonably consent to a masochistic practice need not mean the practice is not torture. Sussman's notion of "reasonable" seems to be nonmoralized, as Johann Frick pointed out. That is, it does not assume that preventing A from impermissibly killing B is a purpose A could reasonably share just because it is a correct purpose.

33. These remarks are a response to Arthur Ripstein's concern that we often are not at liberty to do what is better for someone when we only have his permission to act in the nonoptimal way.

34. This objection was raised by Christine Korsgaard (on the assumption that slavery, understood as forced labor, can be better than death).

35. For more on the importance of holding all factors constant when testing the moral significance of a particular contrasting pair of factors, see my *Morality, Mortality, Vol. 2* (New York: Oxford University Press, 1996).

36. Thomas Nagel (in his "War and Massacre," *Philosophy & Public Affairs* 1 [Winter 1972]: 123–44) has argued that while it is permissible to kill a soldier in war, it is impermissible to cut off his food or medical supplies or to use chemical weapons so that he is unable to fight. These are impermissible, he thinks, because they attack the soldier as a human being; they are not directed at his aggressive acts per se, even though attacking him as a human being would inhibit his aggressive acts. Suppose that being deprived of food and medicine and being attacked with chemicals is much better for the soldier than death. Further, suppose that as he is attacking us, depriving him of food or medicine or using the chemicals would cause him to stop attacking. It seems to me morally preferable to do this rather than kill him. It is even clearer that it is permissible to do this to a criminal wrongdoer as he acts, if it will stop his act, rather than kill him. (It may not be correct to view opponent soldiers, even fighting for an unjust cause, as mere criminal wrongdoers.)

37. Alex Voorhoeve emphasized this to me. Note that he might not prefer death to a humiliating form of torture, if he would not stop his attack in order to stop the torture. But he might also prefer death just to the humiliating torture itself.

38. I shall here ignore reasons that might stem from an agent's own preference not to kill someone.

39. In *The Journal of Philosophy* 72 (1975): 659–60.

40. I owe this point to Johann Frick.

41. Suppose Herman were right that coercing a person is contrary to the CC test and is a direct attack on agency, while killing a person is contrary to the CW test and is an attack on the conditions of agency. This need not imply that we may not torture an aggressor as a substitute for killing an aggressor. Herman herself, we have seen, argues that killing an aggressor need not run afoul of the CW test. She might also say that torturing (wide or narrow) an aggressor to stop his attack does not run counter to the CC test, though she does not discuss this in "Murder and Mayhem." But to agree with my conclusion that we should sometimes narrow torture rather than kill, she would still have to agree that directly subordinating an aggressor's will is less an offense against a still-valuable rational agent than merely eliminating the condition of his agency by killing him.

42. Let us consider these issues in more detail. Shue thinks that an ideologically committed terrorist will not be able to protect himself from torture by betraying his cause because betrayal for reasons of self-interest would be shameful. Hence, such a terrorist will be defenseless, and Shue thinks this makes it wrong to torture him. (As I have already objected to the relevance of someone's being defenseless for the permissibility of harming him, I shall not be concerned with that point here.) A possible alternative concern with torturing someone who is an ideologically committed terrorist is that it would be morally wrong of him to betray his cause (given that he continues to believe in it, even though it would be morally better if he did not believe in it), and it would be morally wrong for us to try to get him to do this moral wrong. But if the alternative to torturing someone requires getting him to do something morally wrong, there is nothing he may do to defend himself against torture and (supposedly) it is wrong to torture the defenseless. I shall call the first concern the "Inability Concern" and the second concern the "Moral Concern."

Consider the Inability Concern first. (i) As Sussman notes, this concern could not be an objection to torturing a terrorist-for-hire rather than a true believer, and it seems odd to think that Shue would condone the former. (ii) The concern would also not arise if torture led to a completely automatic, involuntary gesture that reveals the crucial information we need to stop a threat. Shue's Inability Concern does not apply to this type of torture because the gesture does not depend on the terrorist's will. (iii) The sense in which some committed terrorists are "unable to give in" and avoid torture is that they refuse to give in because they think that to do so is shameful. However, that some refuse to give in for this reason does not mean that every committed terrorist is unable to act in (what he thinks is) a shameful manner.

Shue thinks that the only solution to the problem of a committed terrorist who "cannot" do something shameful is to offer an escape from torture that is acceptable to him. We do not do this if we give him a choice between only evil options, even when one is greater and the other is lesser. It is an evil to be tortured and it is an evil to behave shamefully, and this, Shue thinks, raises a problem for torturing at least one type of ideologically committed terrorist.

Notice, however, that sometimes the choice we offer someone is not between two evils, and yet the choice might confront him with doing something shameful. This will be true when we tempt someone with something good and the alternative to his taking the good thing involves his just not getting it, rather than an evil such as pain or torture. For example, if we offer an already financially secure terrorist a lot of money to tempt him away from his commitment to his cause, his not getting the money as a result of refusing it is not an evil. Nevertheless, if he gives in, he may be doing something shameful and we will be encouraging him to do so. Furthermore, in this case, it is not true that we do not offer the perpetrator a morally acceptable escape from the evil of doing something shameful since we offer him the opportunity to simply not take the good. Hence, offering inducements seems to satisfy Shue's concern that we give a committed terrorist a morally acceptable option and yet it involves trying to get him to do something shameful.

Those who focus on the Moral Concern would rule out not only torture but also the use of inducements, such as promises of freedom and financial security, in order to get someone to betray a cause in which he believes. (Whether one should keep such a promise to a wrongdoer who gives information raises the issue of whether it is permissible to make a lying promise to someone to stop his threats. I believe this is permissible, especially if killing or torture would be permissible.) They might rule out offering someone a tempting good in return for his not setting a bomb to begin with. Betrayal of a cause for a small reward such as a delicacy, for which we know someone has a special weakness, would be even more shameful than betrayal to avoid much pain. Yet it seems quite permissible to do this to stop a terrorist, contrary to what is predicted by the Moral Concern.

Indeed, I think that it can be morally preferable to use methods that most clearly lead to shameful conduct (such as betraying a cause in which one believes for the sake of small inducements) rather than methods that less clearly lead to shameful conduct (such as giving in to terrible pain). This could be so, even if we are dealing with harm and suffering in torture cases. For example, would it be morally worse to try to get a person to stop his terrorist act (a) by using torture to degree x that breaks the person down to a nonrational, panicked state, or (b) by using torture to the same degree x that leads only to reasons of self-interest overcoming his commitment to his cause? Even though the second course more clearly involves trying to corrupt someone, I think that it could be preferable to reducing someone to a nonrational, panicked state. This is so, even if the corrupted person would be less worthy of respect than the reduced person. The reduced person may still feel shame at having succumbed, but he would be more an object of pity than scorn in the eyes of others.

It might be objected that pain and suffering that lead to a breakdown must be greater than the pain and suffering that give one merely a prudential reason to divulge information (contrary to our hypothetical case), and this is why the former could be prohibited when the latter is not. One way to respond to this objection is to imagine that person M can withstand more pain and suffering than person N can before breaking down. We have a choice of causing the same amount of pain in either M or N in order to stop their actions. It would be morally preferable, I think, to torture M (other things equal). Another alternative is to imagine options involving no pain and suffering at all. For example, as Sussman points out, it is also possible to break down someone by using intense pleasure. The contrast is either to provide intense pleasure that interferes with action or provide intense pleasure that leaves someone able to simply decide in favor of its continuing by, for example, not acting. Giving in, in the second case, arguably reflects worse on someone and raises the Moral Concern to a greater extent, yet it seems morally preferable to breaking someone down.

We could also contrast corrupting someone with producing purely automatic responses without pain, suffering, or pleasure. For example, suppose that we could for a brief duration give someone a truth serum that made it impossible for him to exercise self-control, so that he blurted out anything he knew. The alternative, equally successful way to get information is to bribe the person with the prospect of rewards rather than punishments. I suggest that it is no solution to the moral problem of corrupting someone to instead bypass his rational agency in this way, even without using pain or pleasure.

Why might it be morally preferable to avoid such means as the truth serum (even if they are not always ruled out)? This is a difficult question. I suspect that it may be better in the long run for the person himself to lose control in a way that, in some ways, reduces him to a nonperson level for a short while rather than for him to be corrupted. However, it is contrary to the importance of being a person to try to elicit responses from him by trying to bypass his rational control in this way. Furthermore, those who undermine a person's agency in this way bear full responsibility for his state and what he does in it. The alternative may involve encouraging him to make choices that reflect badly on his character, but the outcome will be a function of his full humanity being exercised, not short-circuited, and more responsibility for the outcome will lie with him. (Sussman suggests [in correspondence] that the answer to why it might be morally more appropriate to corrupt rather than use a truth serum that involves no fear or pain may be different from the answer to why it might be better to corrupt through pain rather than break down someone in the same way.)

43. It might be proposed that it is wrong to call some torture "permissible" just because doing it is morally preferable to some other act. Ours might be the sort of dilemma where whatever we do is wrong. But I do not think this can be correct. After all, killing A is assumed to be permissible if it were our only option. So if substituted torture were wrong, we could kill instead. Yet it seems wrong to kill rather than torture.

44. I discuss this issue in some more detail in describing what I call the Principle of Secondary Permissibility (PSP). See *Intricate Ethics*.

45. I try to describe these matters in greater detail in *Intricate Ethics*.

46. It might also be suggested that it is in A's interest to be tortured rather than to kill B impermissibly. One interpretation of this claim supposes that we are certain that he would be captured and executed if he kills B. Then the case in which we could only torture to stop his act could also be thought of as a case in which we torture him rather than kill him after he is captured. However, another, moralized interpretation of the claim is that even if A would escape execution, we do him a service in preventing him from being a murderer.

47. This is a case presented by Jeff McMahan in his *Killing in War* (Oxford: Clarendon Press, 2009). Following McMahan (for the most part), I take "being liable" to imply that someone has no complaint if something is done to him to which he is liable. Liability is distinct from desert, as someone can be liable to be harmed even if he does not deserve to be harmed. I take desert to imply that there is a positively good feature of a state of affairs if someone gets what he deserves. This need not be the case if someone gets that to which he is liable. Also, someone's being liable to harm need not be necessary in order for it to be permissible to harm him. It could be permissible to engage in an activity that harms someone when the person harmed still has a complaint if he is harmed and may be entitled to compensation. (For distinctions along these lines, see *Killing in War*.) Many think that even a so-called "innocent threat," who is both inactive and not responsible for being an unjust threat, is permissibly subject to being attacked. For example, suppose an innocent person is hurled at a trigger that would set off a bomb that kills someone else. Many think it is permis-

sible to kill this innocent threat to stop his falling on the trigger, even though his threatening movement is not an act of his. I have suggested that an innocent threat owes it to his potential victim to divert himself from his potential victim, if he can, though at costs that are not necessarily as high as those that might be imposed on him by others to stop his falling on the trigger. (For example, he may have a duty to suffer a broken leg to divert himself but not death, and yet he might be killed by others if necessary to stop his falling on the trigger.) For more on these issues, see my *Creation and Abortion* (New York: Oxford University Press, 1992) and "The Insanity Defense, Innocent Threats, and Limited Alternatives," *Criminal Justice Ethics* 6 (1987): 61–7.

48. He may be excused for not doing these things, given how hard they would be to do, but that is consistent with his having an obligation to do them.

49. Suppose it made sense to have public law declare torture to be legally impermissible, even while recognizing that sometimes it would be morally permissible. It might be argued that if it is ever morally permissible to violate the law, it is to do a morally obligatory, not merely a morally permissible, act. If this were so, then torturing would have to be morally obligatory for certain public officials in order for them to be justified in disobeying the law. However, it is also possible that when a person is willing to do a supererogatory act, the fact that justice calls for the act may be enough to justify his violating the law. (After all, not all justifiably civilly disobedient agents had a moral duty to do the acts [such as sitting at lunch counters] that broke unjust laws.)

50. This is true, even though if we are certain he will be successful, doubts that A is trying to kill B need not affect our willingness to kill A if this is necessary to stop his act of killing B.

51. See Jeff McMahan, "Torture in Principle and in Practice," *Public Affairs Quarterly* 22 (April 2008): 91–108. McMahan there, independently, argues that it is permissible to torture to stop a killer's act.

52. Julian Savulescu suggests another alternative: The right not to be tortured is simply trumped by the right of the innocent person not to be killed. I think that the fact that we do not owe compensation to the aggressor for harm done to him suggests that his right is not "intact," and so the trumping really involves a specification of the right (something internal to the right) or occurs because the right is already weakened.

53. The conceptual issue should not unnecessarily distract us, however interesting it is in its own right. For suppose it was incorrect to apply the term

"torture" to treatment during an aggressive act. Then we could simply define "schmorture" as "treatment otherwise like torture, except that it occurs during the aggressive act." The normative question would be whether some "schmorture" is permissible, and if it is, what bearing this has on the permissibility of torture (defined as not occurring during an aggressive act).

54. In comments on an earlier version of this chapter.

55. Below, I shall offer a suggestion for why people tend to focus on ticking bomb cases.

56. I have considered only short periods of intense pain in the Killer Cases that would still be sufficient to be called torture (whether wide or narrow). I have considered whether such torture is sometimes permissible. Suppose not all types of torture are permissible, for example, as a "lesser evil" substitute for killing. Then must those who argue that some forms of torture are sometimes permissible show how to draw a line between the permissible and impermissible forms? This is an important project, but I do not think it is necessary in order to show that sometimes torture is permissible. It is said that we can tell the difference between morning and night without being able to say where dusk begins and ends. It would similarly be wrong to argue that just because we do not yet know where permissible torture changes into impermissible torture that we cannot tell that some instances are permissible.

57. "During his act" might be taken to imply that the person is a responsible agent throughout the duration of his act. But it is useful to note that we can imagine cases in which someone is morally responsible for making himself at t_1 into an "automaton" at the time t_2 when he "acts." For example, suppose A is afraid that he will suffer weakness of will at the time he is to kill B. He takes a drug that makes it henceforth impossible for him not to kill B. (Or he takes a drug that makes it henceforth impossible for him not to kill B unless we are able to trigger him into doing another type of movement.) I do not think that A's not being a morally responsible agent throughout his act makes it impermissible to kill or torture him (in the manner described in the Killer Cases) in order to stop his killing B. This is because he is morally responsible for making it the case that he engages in an "act" of killing while not morally responsible.

58. In some other cases, we cannot prevent the harm to B, but we can make it possible to undo this harm only by doing something to A during his attack that will shortly kill him. For example, we could imagine that only

shooting a bullet into A while he is attacking B will lead to a device being available to operate on B, and this is the only way to save B from A's attack. Could doing this to A be permissible? It might be argued that it is important to prevent A's harming B because it is important that B not be in a harmed state as a result of A's act. One way to prevent B's being in a harmed state is to prevent his being harmed in the first place, even if this requires killing A to stop his act or its effects. But, it may be asked, why may we not prevent B's being in a harmed state by doing something to A while he acts that allows us to undo the harm to B subsequently? I first discussed related issues in "The Insanity Defense, Innocent Threats, and Limited Alternatives." There I was concerned with what we may do to individuals who actively harm others (or have been made into threatening objects) *after they have caused harm* in order to undo the harm. This is different from what we may do to them while they attack in order to help their already harmed victims.

59. Warren Quinn, "Actions, Intentions, and Consequences: The Doctrine of Double Effect," in his *Morality and Action* (New York: Cambridge University Press, 1994), p. 186.

60. Even if it were not permitted to kill A in Killer Case (5), we could use the direct proportionality argument discussed in Section II to try to justify the torture.

61. What was said in n. 53 above is also relevant at this point.

62. We will consider another conception of an action below.

63. I shall not here include under "ex post torture" torture that would occur after a victim has been harmed, in order to either undo or compensate for the harm. I considered the issue of whether we could harm a wrongdoer for these purposes in my "The Insanity Defense, Innocent Threats, and Limited Alternatives."

64. Some may argue that torture can only occur in such a case and none of the cases I have described previously involved torture. I think this would be to inappropriately restrict the term, perhaps in an attempt to make it involve only morally impermissible acts. Again, what was said in n. 53 above is also relevant.

65. As noted earlier, it is part of Shue's argument against torturing captives that it is impermissible to torture someone who is no longer a threat to anyone. He contrasts this with the permissibility of even killing combatants who are threats. This contrast with what it is permissible to do to combatants may evoke the thought that when combatants are captured

and are prisoners of war, it is impermissible to torture or otherwise harm them. However, this limitation may apply only to those who serve in the military service of a country engaged in a standard war, where all warring parties are subject to this convention on the treatment of prisoners of war. A killer or terrorist who is captured may not be such a prisoner of war—certainly if A were an ordinary criminal he would not be—and so how it is morally permissible to treat him might have to be settled independently of a convention about prisoners of war. In addition, harm to combatants after they have been captured may be ruled out because it would only be punishment. By contrast, in the cases we are considering, the ex post torture is used as a means of saving the potential victim of the person to be tortured, not as punishment.

66. We are, of course, not discussing ex post punishment.

67. Ordinarily, we might explain the limits on what may be done to wrongdoers ex post (aside from punishment) by the fact that threatening to harm a wrongdoer to get him to desist would be ineffective, if it was known that he could be harmed even after desisting. But the cases we are dealing with specifically involve situations in which once an act ends, the threat to a victim is not over. Hence, nothing of benefit to victims is gained by ruling out ex post harm to a wrongdoer. It may also be true that ordinarily harming during an act is more likely to be effective in stopping harm to a victim than harm ex post. However, in our cases, we are assuming away this difference so it cannot account for any residual resistance to ex post harm.

68. See my brief discussion of this point earlier, pp. 15–16.

69. We could also imagine (as in Section III) that we interfere at the time of his still presenting the threat (only now this includes his refraining from aid) without stopping his presenting it. That is, we only stop the success of the attack and/or the harm it would cause.

70. Whether or not a wrongdoer in captivity is still presenting a threat of death or physical harm to his original victims, it is worth noting that he may be engaged in torturing those who consider torturing him. What I have in mind depends on the idea of psychological torture. It is said that torture includes telling someone that either he or people he cares about will be killed if he does not do something. Imagine a terrorist who knows that a bomb will shortly go off—either because he started it or just because he knows of others who started it—unless a country or its agents change their behavior. The terrorist might constantly repeat this information to his

captors, who cannot avoid contact with him, when these captors (or their loved ones) would be killed by the bomb. The terrorist seems to be psychologically torturing his captors.

71. It might be suggested that a different argument for the moral significance of ex postness is based on the fact that during an act, torture only interferes with an act, whereas ex post torture coercively tries to change someone's will so that he acts differently. But we have described cases in which coercive torture (i.e., torture-narrow) would be applied during an act to get someone to alter his action. (See pp. 13 and 20.) If doing this is permissible, it cannot be the distinction between torture-wide and torture-narrow that accounts for the significance of ex postness. Furthermore, there could be ex post cases in which torture-wide would elicit movements that stop a threat. If torture-wide is impermissible ex post, it cannot be the distinction between torture-wide and torture-narrow that accounts for the moral significance of ex postness.

72. This suggestion is made by Gerald Lang in his review of *Ethics and Humanity: Themes from the Philosophy of Jonathen Glover*, eds. N. Ann Davis et al. (Oxford: Oxford University Press, 2010) in *Philosophical Reviews* (online), 8/11/2010. I am grateful to Julie Tannenbaum for drawing my attention to Lang's discussion.

73. I think this distinction is less plausible when someone deliberately presents a threat to someone, as in the Killer Cases.

74. Similar questions can be raised about nonactive innocent threats. It was said that losses that may be imposed on them during their harmful movement could be larger than ones they would have to impose on themselves to stop their threatening movement. (See n. 47.) If the nonactive innocent threat landed on the trigger, starting the bomb which has not yet exploded, may losses be demanded of or imposed ex post upon the person who was the nonactive innocent threat (in particular) to stop the bomb? Intuitively, it seems that he is more immune from such ex post costs than the innocent driver who was at least responsible for deciding to drive.

75. We have earlier (in n. 42 above) considered the view that the aid might not be easy, in various senses.

76. He also does not refuse to allow himself to be shocked so that he could rescue B. I raise this point because Sussman's remarks (in personal communication) suggest that he thinks that whether A refused to let himself be shocked so that he could aid is morally relevant to whether it is permissible to shock him. But it is hard to see how A's refusal to be shocked

could be grounds for the permissibility of shocking him, if he was not already liable to the shocks that he refused.

77. On Sussman's view, refraining means A is still presenting a threat. Hence, if narrow-torturing were permissible, this would not show that narrow-torturing someone who has finished presenting a threat and did not refrain from aid is permissible.

78. It might be said that one reason we should not torture post-act someone who is not wrongfully refraining from aid is that someone may regret his action and even have become a reformed person post-act. (Ralph Wedgwood raised this point.) Such facts, I think, might be relevant to whether we should punish an agent post-act. But we are not concerned here with punishment. We are only concerned with whether we may sometimes torture someone when this would help his victim avoid harm. It might be said that a wrongdoer who has reformed should recognize his responsibility to his victim in virtue of his initial act—that would be part of his reforming. If he is unconscious and is not able to recognize his responsibility, that does not affect his having the responsibility.

79. This should be true even if we are more likely to save B by torturing C than A. Hence, it is not the mere usefulness for bringing about a good consequence, nor just any sort of wrongdoing that affects whether B survives, that justifies torture.

80. Of course, it could be morally preferable to do something to A after his act rather than during it if we had the choice, because less harm to A is required ex post in order to save B than would be required during A's act. For example, it might be morally preferable to refrain from killing A, when killing him would be necessary to stop his setting a bomb that will kill B, if one knows for certain that one can stop the bomb before it goes off by doing less harm to A ex post. This, however, is a case in which we would substitute one act for another because it is in the interest of the person we would harm. It does not directly bear on a case in which we could only stop the success of someone's threat ex post.

81. As suggested by David Sussman in his comments on an earlier version of this chapter. Sussman's suggestion seems to imply that the perpetrator should agree to (what we would ordinarily call) torture and is only subject to our torturing against his will because he does not consent. See also n. 76 above.

82. It is often said that hypothetical cases that involve torturing ex post a known terrorist in order to certainly stop a threat that we know he started

and that will certainly cause much harm are unrealistic. It is said that we could never have such perfect knowledge. My point here is that we may also not have such perfect knowledge in other cases, such as a version of Killer Case (1), and yet we would think it is sometimes permissible to torture in those other cases.

83. Focusing on cases involving thousands of people does *not* suggest that an act-consequentialist justification of torture is being offered. This is because act consequentialism should permit torture so long as the good produced outweighs the bad, and this might occur if only a small group of victims were saved. However, a rule consequentialist justification of some torture might permit it only when thousands of lives are at stake. This is because a rule consequentialist might be concerned that torturing too frequently, even when it is justified on act consequentialist or even nonconsequentialist grounds (such as I have been considering), might weaken resistance to torturing when it is impermissible. (Derek Parfit reminded me that Richard Hare argued on these grounds against allowing torture.) This concern might be put aside only when very many lives are at stake.

84. This was the version of the agent-focused objection presented by David Rodin in his lecture, "Torture, Rights, and Values: Why the Prohibition of Torture is Absolute," Carnegie Council, July 8, 2008.

85. I am grateful to Ruth Chang, Barbara Herman, Shelly Kagan, Christine Korsgaard, David McCarthy, Jeff McMahan, Derek Parfit, Arthur Ripstein, Julian Savulescu, Larry Temkin, and Alex Voorhoeve for comments on an earlier version of this essay. I am especially grateful for comments from David Sussman. I also received very helpful comments from audiences at Oxford University (where this chapter was presented in November 2008 as one of three Uehiro Lectures), the University of Arizona Philosophy Department, the Ethics Centre, University of Toronto, the Safra Ethics Center Joint Seminar, Harvard University, and the Department of Philosophy, University of California, Los Angeles.

2

TERRORISM AND INTENDING EVIL

My aim in this chapter is to examine some distinctions that may bear on the characterization and morality of terrorism.[1] I start with a rough description of what I call Standard Terrorism (which I shall abbreviate as Terrorism). This is not meant to be a set of necessary and sufficient conditions, but only characteristics that we tend to associate with current terrorism. I will then consider several proposals for why Terrorism is wrong, including the possible distinctiveness of terror, the fact that victims are civilians, the fact that an agent intends to produce the harm and terror, and the fact that there is no military purpose involved. I shall argue that these proposals are inadequate. In particular, I argue that terror is not the most serious part of the wrong of Terrorism and that the intention of the agent is not what makes his act wrong. To support the latter claim, I shall consider cases in which acts are either not Terrorism or remain permissible even when an agent intends harm and terror. I shall then offer an alternative characterization of the most serious part of the wrong of Terrorism. However, I shall also consider some factors that could sometimes make Terrorism permissible. Finally, I shall try to draw some implications of my discussion for "real world" policy. Although this last part of the discussion may not add anything in purely philosophical terms, it seems appropriate for a moral philosopher whose work bears on public policy to suggest ways in which public pronouncements and rules could be made more accurate.

Throughout, I consider the conceptual issue—whether something is an instance of Terrorism and whether some factor is sufficient or necessary for Terrorism to be present—as well as the moral issue—what makes Terrorism most seriously wrong. It is important to remember that the factors that distinguish Terrorism from other types of acts may not account for why it is most seriously wrong. It might be properties it shares with other acts that make it most seriously wrong.

I. *Characterization*

The following is a rough characterization of Terrorism (not a set of necessary and sufficient conditions). The victim is typically a civilian noncombatant (which I shall abbreviate as Civilian) and someone who is not otherwise shortly to die.[2] The bad (broadly construed) that happens to the Civilians in Terrorism is (1) death or grave injury to some; and (2) terror in other Civilians (due to [1]), who are afraid of death or grave injury to themselves or others. The terrorist is a non-state agent, not engaged in standard war between nation-states. This agent intends, rather than merely foresees, the harm and terror to his victims, either as a means or as an end in itself. His actions are also thought through rather than impulsive. If he does not intend the harm and terror as an end in itself (e.g., as punishment), further aims of the terrorist could be political or religious. He might simply be aiming to show the mighty that they are vulnerable. He might be trying to create political pressure by the populace on its government, or directly pressure the opponent government, in order to change that government's policies.[3]

My characterization of Terrorism leaves it open that it might be ultimately justified sometimes, although it is prima facie (or pro tanto) morally wrong, by which I mean impermissible.[4] (I shall use "prima facie" to encompass both types of wrong, unless otherwise noted.)

II. *Accounts of Wrongness*

A. NONSTATE AGENT

What makes Terrorism at least prima facie impermissible? Some focus on the agent being a nonstate actor. However, state-sponsored terrorism could be as morally wrong, even if it were Nonstandard Terrorism. Hence, that a nonstate acts is not enough to account for the serious wrongness of Terrorism.

B. KILLING AND TERROR ITSELF

The obvious objection to Terrorism is that it involves killing Civilians who pose no threat to their attackers or others.[5] It might be said, however, that even if it were permissible to kill such persons, it would still be impermissible to cause them terror, especially for purposes of manipulating political outcomes. It might even be said that terror per se is worse than death. Are these last two claims true?

On one understanding of terror, it is fear of harm (to self or others) that gives those who are terrorized a reason of prudence or altruism, for example, to end a policy to which the terrorist objects. I agree that it is ordinarily wrong to induce such fear in people even as a side effect, and that inducing such fear in some people adds something bad to just killing other people. When one intentionally induces such fear in order to change people's conduct, one will also be engaged in coercively affecting their will. But I do not agree that such fear is, by itself, as great or a greater harm than dying or that intentionally inducing it for coercive purposes is as serious a wrong as the killing.[6] This is, in part, because from any individual's perspective, death is a greater evil than a fear of death.

It might be said that when such fear is widespread in a large population, the aggregated fear in the population is a greater evil than the great loss suffered by an individual who is killed. Aggregating in this way does not seem morally right; after all, no one of the many who are terrorized in this way suffers a loss anywhere near as great as the loss to the person killed, and the wrong done to the person killed is much graver than the wrong done to any individual of the large population who is only made fearful. This is what seems morally relevant.[7]

Some might believe that terror is worse than death because it could lead people to change a correct policy from fear, and doing something in this way is shameful and could be worse than death. If terrorizing people still leaves them a choice about how they will respond, they could become morally responsible for shamefully changing their policy. However, I do not think that having this effect on one's opponent is necessarily a reason why terrorism is impermissible. In a serious conflict, it is too much to ask one side to shield its opponent from shameful choices or bad reasoning. After all, offering great benefits as inducements to change a correct policy might also prompt shameful choices, yet offering such inducements could be permissible in a conflict, even if killing were not permissible.[8]

On a second understanding of terror, it is a form of panic that undermines rational judgment and agency. Individuals surrender once their judgment is undermined, not through an exercise of judgment involving a prudential or altruistic calculation (as in the first form of terror).[9] (One might add that terrorist panic is associated with unpredictable killings of unpredictable targets, and so with the undermining of order necessary for civil society.[10]) Suppose the second understanding of terror better accounts for its evil. Are the panic and disorder really greater evils than the deaths of those killed? Is causing the type of terror that undermines rational agency and order among Civilians as serious a moral wrong as killing Civilians? I do not think so, at least if these effects are temporary and do not result in further deaths.

To consider a case that supports this claim, imagine that we find out that Civilians, whom we would not harm in any other way, will experience terror (of either type), leading to their country's changing its policies, if we bomb some rotting trees. This is because they will believe that we are bombing people. (Call this the Trees Case.) If we do only this to produce terror, this will be a case of Nonstandard Terrorism. The only other way to produce the same change in policies is to actually secretly kill some of these Civilians (so terror in others does not result). I think it is morally preferable to terrorize than to kill.

So when we compare causing either type of terror on its own with killing, the latter is the graver wrong. Is it possible that when terrorizing some accompanies killing others, there is an interaction effect that either makes terrorizing an even graver wrong than killing or diminishes the wrongness of killing? I see no reason to believe this. Hence, I conclude that even though terror adds to the wrong of Terrorism, the major moral obstacle to Terrorism is the killing rather than the production of terror (of either type) or the attempt to manipulate a population for political purposes.[11]

C. CIVILIAN VICTIMS

I shall take it, therefore, that those who ask why Terrorism is seriously wrong are really concerned with why it may be prima facie wrong to kill (including seriously harm) in Terrorism, even when other forms of killing, such as in self-defense, have been justified.

One proposal is that it is the victim's being a Civilian who has not, does not, and will not threaten harm to others that accounts for the prima facie wrongness of Terrorism. Some may suggest, however, that voters who support a policy are liable to being attacked in virtue of indirectly authorizing combatant activities.[12] To avoid this issue, we may imagine that the Civilians killed are nonvoters (e.g., babies, children, and other people) who have no control over their country's policies.

All of this harm to Civilians, however, could also occur as a mere side effect, foreseen or not, of nonterrorist attacks, that is, as collateral damage. For example, the deaths could be side effects of attacks on military targets prompted by military aims, and other Civilians could be terrorized by these deaths. Indeed, it could be terror in response to the collateral deaths of others that causes people to pressure their government into changing policies.[13] Here is a hypothetical example of collateral damage. Suppose that the United States was conducting ongoing military operations against Al Qaeda and that it was instrumentally useful for Al Qaeda to attack the World Trade Center (WTC) because (contrary to fact) it was a center of US military operations and there were no Civilians in it. Suppose also that Civilians killed near the building and the terror resulting from the attack were mere foreseen side effects. (Call this the WTC–Military Case.) Suppose the collateral deaths of Civilians contribute to making an attack on the military WTC impermissible. Would this attack still be a less serious wrong than Terrorism whose effects are identical but in which the Civilians deaths and terror are intended? Could acts with collateral damage to Civilians sometimes be permissible when Terrorism is not (holding constant the harm and terror produced)?[14]

D. INTENTION

The next proposal as to what factors make Terrorism prima facie wrong aims to provide an answer to these questions. It has been claimed that an agent's intending harm and terror as a means or an end, rather than causing them while merely foreseeing them, helps make Terrorism prima facie wrong. There is a separate but related claim that the fact that harm to some Civilians causes terror in others and this terror in turn achieves other goals such as policy change (rather than the harm and terror being mere side effects) helps make Terrorism prima facie wrong.

What is known as the Doctrine of Double Effect (DDE) claims that when an agent intends the harm/terror as a means or an end in itself, and causes it or allows it to occur for these purposes, the agent's act is impermissible.[15] (On some interpretations, the DDE also condemns actions that have a causal role for harm and terror in bringing about goals independent of whether the causal role is intended.[16]) When the same harm and terror are mere (foreseen) side effects, they do not make an act impermissible if they are proportional to the good to be achieved by the act and that act (of all permissible acts) is necessary to achieving the good. Hence, sometimes the DDE rules out acts that cause merely foreseen harm because the harm is out of proportion to a good to be achieved. Yet, it is often said that doing such an act would still not be as serious a wrong as doing an act aiming at the harm, other things equal.

In the rest of this section, I shall explore this view that the agent's intentions determine the impermissibility of Terrorism. I shall also explore how intention relates to necessary and sufficient conditions for Terrorism. Among the general conclusions for which I shall argue are that:

- There is good reason to think that a nonstate agent producing harm and terror to Civilians, against their interest and without their consent, with the intention to do so, even in order to change or protest policies, is not a sufficient condition for the existence of Terrorism. (It may be a necessary condition.)
- When an act is otherwise morally permissible despite the harm and terror it produces, intending the harm and terror as means or ends need not affect the permissibility of the act, contrary to the DDE.
- When the act is otherwise impermissible, intending the harm and terror as means or ends might sometimes, but not always, make the impermissible act be a more serious wrong.

I should note that I believe that one problem with the DDE is that it incorrectly implies that the occurrence of an unintended and proportionate bad side effect of a necessary means to a greater good could not, by itself, be a ground for the impermissibility of an act. This is a serious problem for the DDE, but I shall ignore it here and simply assume that proportionate collateral damage is often permissible.[17]

1. *Conceptual Issues.* I shall begin by considering the purely conceptual question of whether a nonstate agent acting with the intention to harm Civilians as a means to inducing terror in other Civilians, when the terror is intended as a means to change policies, is a sufficient condition for an act to be Terrorism. (I assume Civilians are seriously harmed and terrorized against their self-interest and without their consent.) Consider this question in the following cases, which are variants on ones in which it seems to be permissible to bomb a military facility, causing a certain amount of death and terror as collateral damage. (I use "P" in designating these cases to indicate that I think they involve permissible acts.)

Consider the following Case P(i). Suppose counterfactually that the United States was controlled by Nazis and, as in the WTC–Military Case, the WTC is the site of only military operations.[18] A Resistance would aim to bomb the WTC and destroy ongoing military operations in it. I assume that this would be morally justified (P) despite some side-effect deaths and terror to nonresponsible Civilians nearby. However, there is no Resistance movement that can bomb the military WTC in the imaginary Nazi-controlled United States. Instead, the bombing is done by a nonstate group that I shall call Baby Killer Nation. It is interested in destroying the Nazis' military operations in the WTC only because this is a means to satisfy its own bad desire to cause harm and terror to babies and children living nearby. They have this as an end, but also as a means to protest Nazi pronatalism.[19] Baby Killer Nation members act on their desire to kill babies only when there is an act in a just cause (such as destroying a Nazi state) that can serve "as a pretext." Baby Killer Nation bombardiers who share these intentions would never perform any acts in bombing the WTC that will cause more side-effect damage than would be caused by bombardiers who lack their bad intentions, for fear of the group failing to retain its pretext and so being subject to international punishment. Hence, I assume throughout that Baby Killer Nation's way to have a pretext always involves its carrying out only bombings that would be permissible if done by the Resistance.[20]

I do not think that Baby Killer Nation's act of bombing the WTC in P(i) should be conceived of as an act of Terrorism. Here is a view that might account for this conclusion: The conditions under which leaders of a group will allow themselves to pursue their intention to harm and terrorize Civilians, and their doing nothing besides what others correctly seeking to destroy a military operation would do without bad intentions, should determine the conceptual category—Terrorism or not—into which the act is placed.[21]

To understand this proposal, it may help to consider an analogue to Case P(i) that I call the Bad Man Trolley Case. If a trolley is headed toward killing five people, many think that it would be permissible (even if not obligatory) for a bystander who wants to save the five to redirect the trolley onto another track, even if it will then kill one other person on that track. Suppose, however, that the bystander is a bad person and he would not act to save the five lives, except that he sees that the one person who will be killed if he redirects the trolley is his enemy. He would also not kill his enemy unless he had a pretext of doing some act that actually helped the five people, for he wants to avoid punishment. He turns the trolley only in order to kill his enemy, but only because—on condition that—his turning the trolley will save the five people, so giving him a justifiable pretext.[22] His turning the trolley in this case should not, I think, be categorized as a murder of his enemy.[23]

In the imaginary case I have considered so far, Baby Killer Nation intends to destroy the Nazi WTC military facility, just as the Resistance would have. Hence, it intends something that is, let us assume, good (or at least appropriate). It may be thought that this is why its act should not be classified as Terrorism.

I do not think that this conclusion is correct. For we may imagine a further variation, P(ii), in which the destruction of the Nazi WTC by Baby Killer Nation is only foreseen and not intended. For example, suppose that what Baby Killer Nation must do in order to kill bystanding babies and cause terror is set off a bomb. It then discovers that setting off this same bomb will, as a side effect, destroy the Nazi WTC. This destruction is not the means to causing the damage and terror that Baby Killer Nation seeks to produce among Civilians; these would be achieved by its bomb alone. We can imagine that the Resistance, too, would have to explode such a bomb in order to destroy the WTC and it is the bomb that would cause the harm and terror to bystanders, not the destruction of the WTC. I shall assume that it would be permissible for the Resistance to cause this collateral damage by use of the bomb.

We can further imagine that Baby Killer Nation would set off the bomb in P(ii) *only on condition* that it also destroys the WTC, so that it has a pretext of doing only the overt act that the Resistance could permissibly do.

In this case, Baby Killer Nation members do not intend to destroy the Nazi WTC, yet I believe that when they do what has this effect, at least when they knew it would have this effect and they acted on condition that it would, their act is not Terrorism. In defense of this conclusion, it might again be said that the conditions under which the group's leaders will allow themselves to pursue their intention to harm and terrorize Civilians, and thus do nothing besides what others seeking to destroy the military operation would do without bad intentions, should determine whether the act falls in the conceptual category of Terrorism.[24]

So far, I have suggested that doing an act that harms and terrorizes Civilians with the intention to harm and terrorize them is not sufficient to make the act fall into the category of Terrorism. Now recall that I mentioned an alternative construal of the DDE that places emphasis not on an agent's intending harm and terror but on whether harm and terror are in the causal route (are means) to an end or instead are just side effects.[25] Consider the causal role/side effect distinction separately from an agent's intention. Suppose that in the military WTC cases, whether the bombing is done by the Resistance or Baby Killer Nation, the harm and terror are in the causal route that leads to the collapse of the Nazis. That is, the Resistance would intend the attack on the military WTC as part of an attempt to ruin Nazi military power, leading to the downfall of the regime. However, before Nazi military power is ruined, Civilians terrorized as a result of collateral damage from bombing the WTC would overthrow the Nazi government, independently of any military effect of the destruction of the WTC.[26] The actual causal significance of harm and terror would not be enough, I think, for Resistance bombings of the WTC to be acts of Terrorism, even were this causal route foreseen by them. After all, the Resistance would, by hypothesis, not be intending the harm and terror and this, I believe, is a necessary condition for Terrorism.

How people will react to what is a side effect of another way for the Resistance to achieve its goal does not determine how we should characterize the Resistance's act.

Baby Killer Nation, of course, does intend the harm and terror; they could even see these as the most desirable route to the Nazis' downfall if that will occur (although they do not really care whether the Nazis are brought down, per se). Would their act be Terrorism because they acted from the intention to cause harm and terror and these were the actual causal route to surrender? I do not think so, at least if destroying the military facility is a condition for their bombing at all and they know that the destruction of the military facility is a legitimate alternative route to the Nazis' downfall. The fact that what they intend to happen (for example, harm and terror leading to the downfall) does happen is not sufficient to make their act Terrorism, at least when they know the act they do should be done by the Resistance (despite the harm and terror and the actual role of these in bringing down the regime).[27]

2. *Moral Issues.* I now turn to the moral rather than conceptual significance in these cases of an agent's intention to harm and terrorize. (I shall return to the conceptual issue eventually.)

Acts that are otherwise right or permissible lack moral worth (in the Kantian sense) when the intention with which they are done is wrong. The complex event of "acting from bad intention" is also worse than an act done from a good intention because there are morally wrong attitudes present. The wrong intention can also reasonably be resented by the people toward whom it is directed (although this does not mean that they have a right that it not exist). Someone concerned about the agent can also wish he did not have the wrong intention for the sake of his own character.

However, all this does not imply that the intention makes an act impermissible when another act like it in all respects, except for stemming from a different intention, is permissible. The most straightforward reason for this is the following: When an agent has a wrong intention, he does not do an act for the sake of the properties that make the act permissible or required—he acts for a bad reason—but that need not make the act itself lose any of the properties that make it permissible or required. This is shown, as Thomas Scanlon has argued, by the fact that in most cases an agent can decide whether an act is permissible or required by considering properties and effects the act would have independently of considering with what intention she would do the act.[28]

Furthermore, we ordinarily think that the primary reason why an act that harms and terrorizes people is a wrong act is that it has properties to whose existence those people would be justified in objecting on their own behalf, in the sense that the properties would give them a right to have the act not be done. I have said that victims could reasonably resent the bad intention of the Baby Killer Nation agent (if babies attacked were capable of resentment) because of the attitude to them it expresses, but this would not necessarily give them a right that he not so intend. Could they rightfully object to the occurrence of harm and terror that the agent causes them, just because he did not do the act that brings about the harm and terror for the sake of destroying Nazi munitions? When even his victims (if reasonable) should agree that destruction of the munitions actually justifies doing an act that causes them harm and terror, do they have a right that he not act unless he acts for the right reason (or at least for a reason that they do not justifiably resent)?

I believe, in the cases we have considered, that the potential victims have no such right and that they can point to no grounds affecting them as sufficient reasons why the act should not be done. They have no right that the agent not bomb merely so that his wrong intention not lead to the bombing that harms them. The victims have no right that the agent not do an act that harms and terrorizes them unless it is done for unobjectionable reasons when his act has the effect that justifies harm and terror to them (i.e., destroying Nazi munitions), at least when he takes that effect as a condition of his act and all other effects are the same as they would be if the Resistance acted.[29] It is possible that some effects of an act will differ depending on an agent's intentions. For example, a bad agent's happiness is a probable effect of his causing harm to civilians. By contrast, a good agent's appropriate misery is a probable effect of his causing harm. However, in our case I do not think that the addition of an agent's inappropriate happiness to the outcome of his act is a sufficient reason for its victims having a right that the act not be done, given the other outcomes of the act.[30] It is in this sense that they cannot reasonably object to the agent acting, and it is at least in this sense that the act is not impermissible.

Hence, we need not require Baby Killer Nation or its pilots to refrain from doing what blows up the military target, even when we know that they will act only with the wrong intention. This is true even if we should not permit acts that would destroy the Nazi regime but are prima facie impermissible on grounds other than the agent's intentions. That is, in allowing Baby Killer Nation to act, we need not merely be following a policy of allowing any prima facie impermissible act just because it helps achieve the greater good of destroying the Nazi regime.

Recall that in some of the cases I have presented, Baby Killer Nation does intend to destroy the Nazi WTC. Some may think that so long as the agent is intending such a good (or at least appropriate) thing (even as a mere means to harm and terror) his act is permissible, whatever his further intention. However, we also imagined another case, P(ii), in which the destruction of the Nazi WTC is not intended by Baby Killer Nation, but only a foreseen side effect of its bombing, and it takes advantage of the destruction as a pretext that allows it to pursue its aims. Yet, I believe, its setting off this bomb that kills and terrorizes and also destroys the WTC is permissible. I conclude that an intention to do something good or appropriate need not accompany an intention to cause harm and terror in order that an act be permissible. If I am right, our cases show not only that the DDE is wrong in claiming that the intention to cause harm and terror makes an act impermissible, but that it is wrong if it claims that an intention to do something good or appropriate (either as an end or a means) is necessary in order for the good that is caused by what we do to justify a bad effect. For example, Baby Killer Nation in P(ii) does not intend anything good and yet the good it does could justify lesser harm that is an effect of its acts.[31]

It remains to consider the moral significance of the causal role/side effect distinction separately from the intention/foresight distinction. Does it become impermissible to bomb the Nazi military facility, whose destruction could have helped bring about Nazi surrender for purely military reasons, just because the actual causal route to Nazi surrender will be through harm and terror? I do not think that it is impermissible to destroy a military facility whose destruction would end Nazi rule and also justify collateral deaths and terror (when refraining would allow Nazi rule to continue), just because (one foresees that) Civilian response to the deaths and terror will actually cause Nazis' downfall. In particular, the addition of an actual causal role for harm and terror does not make the outcome so much worse that it would make the Resistance bombing the military facility impermissible. Whether or not it was intended that this causal role occur, it was not necessary that it be the route to the Nazis' downfall; bombing the military facility would have done that too, and this, when collateral damage is proportional, is sufficient to make the act justified. (This is all on the assumption we have made that sometimes harm and terror are tolerable side effects of producing a greater good or of means to it.[32])

3. *More Conceptual Issues.* Now let us return to the conceptual issue of whether certain properties are sufficient to make an act Terrorism. Suppose, contrary to what I suggested earlier, Baby Killer Nation Cases P(i) and P(ii) should be categorized as Terrorism. A possible rationale for the switch in categorizing is that in virtue of the intention to harm and terrorize, a *meaning* of Baby Killer Nation's bombing of the WTC is that they seek to destroy and terrorize civilians as an end in itself or as a means.[33] It might be suggested that we should apply "Terrorism" to acts that have these meanings, whether or not the victims know that this is their meaning. (Call this the Meaning Theory of Terrorism.) I argued in (2) that the acts that the Meaning Theory labels Terrorist are permissible. Hence, if the Meaning Theory is correct, there are permissible acts of Terrorism. (This does not mean that the aspects of these acts that make them Terrorism are not wrong or that these aspects make the acts permissible.)

Furthermore, on the Meaning Theory of Terrorism, it will turn out that some permissible acts of Terrorism are justified by even small good effects. This will be so if the act that causes harm and terror is a necessary, legitimate means to a small, good effect, not relying on any causal route to this good effect through the harm and terror, and the collateral harm and terror that result are proportionate to the good achieved. For example, suppose that it is permissible for a nonstate agent to bomb a small Nazi munitions factory whose elimination will diminish Nazi power a bit, even though ten innocent Civilians will be killed as a side effect and a few others will be terrorized. If Baby Killer Nation bombs the factory in order to kill the ten people and terrorize the few others, its act is Terrorism according to the Meaning Theory, even though it does (and would do) only what the Resistance, lacking its wrong intentions, would do. Then it is an implication of what I argued in (2), combined with the truth of the Meaning Theory, that this Terrorist bombing is permissible if destruction of the factory itself is a legitimate means to diminish Nazi power.

I conclude, at this point, that we cannot decide whether acts that are Terrorist according to the Meaning Theory are impermissible without first considering the other possible effects of these acts that could justify them, such as destroying military targets that can cause Nazi surrender, even when the harm and terror caused are both intended and actually causally efficacious in bringing about surrender.[34] I myself do not recommend the Meaning Theory of Terrorism as a correct account of when an act is Terrorism (or Nonstandard Terrorism). Hence, in what follows, I shall not assume that an act is Terrorism simply because it would be according to the Meaning Theory.

4. *Intention and Impermissible Acts.* So far, in considering the possible role of intention in identifying and morally evaluating Terrorism, we have discussed what seem to be permissible bombings. Now we will consider cases where the bombing seems impermissible (abbreviated as [I]). These include cases where the direct target is inappropriate (for example, it is not a military facility) or because there is nonproportionate collateral damage. We will consider how intention and the actual causal route to good effect through harm and terror affect (i) the type and (ii) seriousness of the wrong done.

(a) In general, in cases where the agent should refrain from his act, it seems more likely that we should refer to his intention to characterize the act's type, even if we do not accept the Meaning Theory in general. I think that this is because an act that should never have been done has no property or effect that justifies it and makes it morally doable as an act of that type. Hence, the type is more likely to be settled by an agent's intention. If this were true, the role of intention in determining the type of act might be different for permissible and impermissible acts.

Nevertheless, the impermissibility of the act can be due to factors other than the intention to harm and terrorize (or any other intention).

Consider how we might reason about the relevance of intention in deciding on the type of a particular impermissible act. Suppose that an agent in a trolley case who intends to kill his six enemies is also helpful and stupid: he would have impermissibly redirected the trolley toward six people in order to save five people, even if the six were not his enemies. Suppose also that the agent would only kill his six enemies because the act that does this saves the five; that is, he wants his killing to coincide with what he (incorrectly) believes is the right act of saving five at the expense of six. Call this the Stupid Man Trolley Case. I suggest that we might then classify the agent's killing of his enemies in the same way that we would classify a simply stupid person's saving of the five at the expense of six, not as murder. This is because the agent appears to have two intentions in the circumstance when he kills the six—to save the five and to kill his enemies—and the first intention is primary in that it suffices on its own as a reason for his action and also sets the condition for his acting on his other intention. Notice that although intention seems to be relevant to how we categorize the act, it is not the intention to kill his enemies that determines the act's category (i.e., murder or impermissible stupidity).

Similarly, imagine a further variant on the hypothetical WTC–Military Case, in which Al Qaeda bombs the WTC military operations in a perfectly just United States, and it also intends the death and terror that occur to bystanding Civilians. Bombing this military operation would be wrong on its own as there is no just cause to attack the United States (by hypothesis). It would also be wrong because it causes disproportionate Civilian harm and terror. Al Qaeda, let us suppose, would have done the wrong of bombing the military WTC in a perfectly just United States, even if Civilians would not have been killed and terrorized, and it would have carried out its intention to kill and terrorize Civilians only when this act coincided with attacking a military facility. This suggests that it has two goals. That is, it intends to kill and terrorize Civilians, and it also intends to destroy the WTC for military purposes. Furthermore, harming and terrorizing Civilians are not necessary for it to act but the possibility of destroying the military WTC is necessary for it to harm and terrorize. If we rely on the Stupid Man Trolley Case as an analogy, we should conclude that in this imaginary case Al Qaeda commits the wrongs of causing disproportionate harm and terror collateral to an impermissible military bombing, not the wrong of Terrorism even though it also intends the harm and terror.

However, this conclusion may be a mistake that arises from focusing too much on the Stupid Man Trolley Case. In that case, the stupid agent responds to a threat to the five that is already occurring and he cannot choose a time to save them when no one is on the other track. But suppose that although Al Qaeda would have bombed the military WTC at t_1 when this would have only destroyed the building, it would have also put off bombing from t_1 to t_2 if it could also kill and terrorize Civilians at t_2. (This would be analogous to a Stupid Man Trolley Case in which the stupid agent delayed saving the five until his six enemies were on the track.) Then the facts that Al Qaeda would have destroyed the military facility on its own, if that were all it could do, and that it acts on its intention to kill and terrorize Civilians conditional on destroying the military WTC, do not show that there is no Terrorism. This is because Al Qaeda, in this imaginary case, could have achieved its (impermissible) military goal at t_1 without killing anyone but it chose not to. So Al Qaeda does not do only what someone who lacked the intention to harm and terrorize but was interested in military victory would have done, namely, bomb the military WTC at t_1 instead of t_2.[35]

However, suppose that it was not possible to select a time to hit the military WTC when no Civilians nearby would be harmed. Then the fact that Al Qaeda would do even an impermissible act of bombing a military facility in a just United States with the intention to harm and terrorize Civilians need not imply that its act is Terrorism. This is so if it also intends the impermissible act of destroying a military facility, that intention would have been sufficient for its act, and it is a condition of pursuing its other intention to harm and terrorize.

Now suppose that there were an actual causal route to surrender through harm and terror. Put very briefly, I think this has no effect on determining whether the impermissible act is Terrorism, for the same reasons (given above) that it had no effect on determining the category of a permissible act.

(b) Does the intention to harm and terrorize make an act that is wrong (on grounds other than the intention of the agent) a more serious wrong? This may be so, as intention to harm seems to be what makes first-degree murder a more serious wrong than second-degree murder. If this is true, it would help show that Terrorism or Nonstandard Terrorism that involves an intention to harm and terrorize can be a more serious wrong than wrongfully causing the same amount of harm and terror as collateral damage. It would also show that even when intention cannot make what is otherwise a permissible act into an impermissible one, it can affect how serious a wrong an impermissible act is. However, suppose an agent acts on the intention to harm and terrorize only when he can also do a wrong act that accomplishes another wrong intention he has, and he would have done the wrong act from the second intention even if, counterfactually, no harm and terror had been produced. Then, I believe, doing the wrong act with an intention to harm and terrorize would not make the wrong done a more serious wrong. (This is true of the case [p. 88] in which Al Qaeda could pick no other time to bomb the Military–WTC, except when civilian harm and terror it intends will occur.)

Finally, consider whether the actual causal role of harm and terror in achieving an aim affects the seriousness of wrong conduct. If collateral harm and terror make it wrong to bomb a military facility in order to show that one's enemy is vulnerable, will the wrong one does be more serious if it is the harm and terror that are actually causally effective in showing that vulnerability? It is possible that it is a worse outcome for a country to be shown to be vulnerable for one reason (its population is frightened) rather than for another (its military is subject to attack), although this strikes me as implausible. If it *is* possible, and how serious a wrong act is can be a function of how bad an outcome it produces, then a wrong act can be a more serious wrong if it produces such a worse outcome. This can be true even if the additional badness of the outcome would not be enough to turn a permissible act into an impermissible one.

(c) *Implications for 9/11.* What does this tell us about the actual case of bombing the WTC on September 11, 2001 (9/11)? It would not tell us much if it were really important that Civilians involve people who had no responsibility (e.g., by way of voting) for policies that may have been wrong. This is because mostly voting adults were killed on 9/11. I shall ignore this difference between 9/11 and cases we have discussed, assuming, for the sake of this argument, that any political role they had did not make them liable to being killed (even as a side effect). Hence, I shall also refer to a mix of such noncombatant adults, children, and other adults as Civilians. I also assume the act of destruction of the Twin Towers (in which no military operations were ongoing) by itself would have been wrong, and that causing death and terror to Civilians, even as collateral damage, would have been wrong.

Given these assumptions, our previous discussion implies that in order to determine if the wrong act is in the category of Terrorism, we have to consider (a) whether Al Qaeda would have bombed the non-military WTC in order, for example, to show how vulnerable its enemy was, even if no deaths or terror would have occurred, and (b) how it picked the time of its attack. If it chose to bomb when it did only because both destruction of the WTC and harm and terror to Civilians would occur, rather than at another time when only destruction of the WTC would occur, its wrong act was Terrorism rather than impermissibility bombing with impermissible collateral damage.

E. DOING HARM TO PEOPLE

This analysis, however, misses something about 9/11. For in all the hypothetical cases that I have imagined, the harm and terror occurred to Civilians who were near but not inside the WTC. (I framed the cases in this way because I began my discussion by considering the DDE. It has always been a problem in applying the DDE to say whether all harm and terror that are unintended effects of an agent's act should be treated as side effects in the same way. I wanted to concentrate on the sorts of effects—harm to those near but not in a target—that, if not intended, should clearly be treated differently by the DDE from intended effects.) In the actual hit on the WTC, Civilians were in the building at the time. Therefore, independently of the actual hit, we should imagine cases that help us consider this factor.

Even if there was no intention to kill and terrorize people, destroying a building in which they were located might be construed, in the circumstances, as equivalent to destroying the people whose presence overlapped with the building's presence. (I shall call this intratarget killing.) It raises the same problem for the DDE as intentionally driving over a stretch of road in order to get people to the hospital, when an immovable person occupies that stretch. His being hit need not be intended, as it plays no useful role in getting people to the hospital. Yet, when there is physical overlap of one entity (such as the road or building) and another entity (such as people), intending to hit the first entity might be thought to have the same conceptual and moral significance as intending to hit the second entity.[36]

Thomas Nagel (in his "War and Massacre"[37]) tries to avoid relying on the DDE and the intention/foresight distinction in drawing moral distinctions about conduct in war. Instead, he emphasizes the distinction between "what we do to someone" and "what happens to someone as a result of what we do." For example, he argues that bombing a whole area intending to kill only combatants is impermissible if they are mixed in with Civilians, even if one does not intend to kill the Civilians. He says this is because in bombing, we will still be doing something to the Civilians. Nagel is focusing on what I am calling intratarget killing. His view might also be proposed as another account of what makes Terrorism morally wrong: Civilians die because of what is done to them, not merely as an effect of what is done to someone or something else.

Hence, it might be suggested that the Civilian intratarget damage in Al Qaeda bombing on 9/11 would have altered the bombing's conceptual and moral status, even if agents had not intended Civilian harm and terror. However, is causing intratarget damage as the result of targeting a site ever sufficient grounds for the wrongful act to be Terrorism rather than some other impermissible act? I think it is no more sufficient to make the act Terrorism than ordinary side-effect harm and terror (discussed earlier). Nagel himself does not claim that bombing an entire area also occupied by Civilians in order to kill combatants is Terrorism when it also kills Civilians. The intention to kill Civilians is necessary for an act to be Terrorism. And intratarget harm is not necessary for Terrorism, as bombing a building in order to cause harm to bystanding Civilians, when a direct hit on the Civilians is impossible, could be Terrorism. Hence, I believe, the addition of intratarget killing alone need not lead us to change any of our prior conclusions about when the impermissible act is Terrorism.

It remains possible that "doing something" deadly and terrorizing to Civilians, rather than their dying and being terrorized as an effect of something else we do, accounts for the particular wrongness of Terrorism (along with Nonstandard Terrorism). However, doing something to an empty building in order to cause death and terror among Civilians seems to also have the particular wrongness of Terrorism, but it may not be "doing something" to Civilians in Nagel's sense. And it may be a different and less serious moral wrong to bomb a whole territory, as in Nagel's example, when it is the only way to achieve one's aim of killing combatants than it would be to bomb a building solely in order to kill and terrorize Civilians. Hence I do not think the wrong of Terrorism is captured by "doing something" to Civilians. Still, independent of the issue of Terrorism, that Al Qaeda's bombing harmed Civilians intratarget could play a role in making its act be a more serious wrong than if the harm to Civilians had been extratarget side effects.

F. NO MILITARY USEFULNESS

Thomas Scanlon argues that the traditional prohibition on terror bombing in war can be explained on grounds that it serves no military purpose, not because of wrong intentions (even if they are present). This explanation could as well be offered as another account of the impermissibility of terrorism. He argues that "military purpose" involves reducing munitions and combatant forces, not causing terror to Civilians as a means to surrender. He says,

> In war, one is sometimes permitted to use destructive and potentially deadly force of a kind that would normally be prohibited. But such force is permitted only when its use can be expected to bring some military advantage, such as destroying enemy combatants or war-making materials, and it is permitted only if expected harm to noncombatants is as small as possible, compatible with gaining the relevant military advantage, and only if this harm is "proportional" to the importance of this advantage....If there is no munitions

plant but a bombing raid that would kill the same number of noncombatants would hasten the end of the war by undermining morale, this raid (a pure case of "terror bombing") would be not permissible under the rationale just given.... The death of noncombatants is not rendered a "military advantage" by the fact that it would shorten the war by undermining public morale.... The intention is wrongful because the act intended is wrongful, and the act is wrongful because of its likely consequence. (That is, it will kill noncombatants without achieving a military advantage.)[38]

I do not think the fact that Terrorism achieves no military advantage correctly explains why it is seriously wrong. First, we can imagine cases in which there is a clear military advantage to be achieved only by killing Civilians as a means. Here are some cases outside of standard war between nation states: (a) A nonstate agent bombs Civilians in order to make opponent soldiers, who are the Civilians' family members, distraught so that the opponent is undefended. (b) A nonstate agent bombs Civilians because their burning is the only way to trigger a fire needed to destroy a munitions factory that is near them (Human Tinder Case). (c) A nonstate agent bombs Civilians so that other terrorized Civilians will stampede and thus destroy a crucial military operation going on nearby (Stampede Case).[39] (The Stampede Case, unlike the earlier ones, relies on causing terror in some Civilians to accomplish the military goal.[40]) I do not think it would be permissible to kill Civilians in these cases (assuming there is no supreme emergency).[41]

The quote from Scanlon to which I have been responding concerns whether there is sufficient military advantage to override the prohibition on use of deadly force. However, subsequently,[42] he claims that the crucial issue concerns the distinction between combatants and noncombatants. He says: "Those who believe that there is an important moral difference between tactical bombing and terror bombing need to defend (some version) of the combatant/noncombatant distinction."

This suggests that it would be permissible to engage in a form of Nonstandard Terrorism that involves killing combatants, not for ordinary military advantage by eliminating the threat they present, but to

Table 2:	Ways to win	
	Military advantage	Civilian demoralization
Combatants (C_O)	C_O(MA)	C_O(CD)
(i) stop threat they present		
(ii) use them in other ways		
Civilians (C)	C(MA)	C(CD)

create fear among the Civilian population. So, for example, an enemy may have an endless supply of soldiers so that killing more is not going to help achieve victory militarily. However, killing more might be done in order to create terror and demoralization among Civilians because so many of their loved ones are being killed. Would this be permissible? Another nonstandard form of terrorism could involve a variant on the Stampede Case involving stampeding combatants.

The issue here is whether we may do things to combatants that are like things we may *not* do to Civilians once we put aside responding to the military threats that they, but not Civilians, actually do or will present.[43] If we may *not* do such things to combatants, then the distinction between combatants and Civilians is not as radical as it would be if we could use combatants to create terror. That is, the distinction would depend only on the fact that Civilians present no threats we are trying to stop.

Table 2 illustrates some possible combinations of the two distinctions that Scanlon focuses on.

However, suppose it were permissible to use combatants to create terror. In particular, if it is permissible to harm combatants in order to produce terror in Civilians, this would imply that terrorizing Civilians is an acceptable means to defeating an opponent. Then it would not be clear how the *im*permissibility of harming Civilians in order to produce Civilian terror to defeat an opponent could be explained by such terror not being a proper military advantage. (This was Scanlon's first suggestion.) And if we may do such things to combatants that are not direct responses to the threat they do or will present, the question is why we may not also do them to Civilians. It may be that only if one presents (or will present) a threat (true of combatants but not Civilians) does one become open to harmful use beyond what is necessary to eliminate one's threat.

G. NECESSARY ROLE

I have argued that we cannot determine that an act that harms and terrorizes is prima facie impermissible, in the way Terrorism is, just because it is brought about by someone with an intention to harm and terrorize Civilians (as an end or a means) or because the actual causal route to an outcome is through this harm and terror. Nor can the combination of these factors determine that an act is prima facie impermissible. They also do not settle the conceptual question of whether the act is Terrorism, except on the Meaning Theory (which I do not recommend). I also argued that it is not doing something to Civilians (in Nagel's sense) that is required for Terrorism or that makes it most seriously wrong. Finally, I concluded that absence of military usefulness is not crucial to an act's being Terrorism or to the impermissibility of Terrorism.

However, all I have said need not imply that it is impossible to characterize Terrorism, and so that what helps make it distinctive also accounts for its prima facie impermissibility, while an act that causes similar harm and terror as foreseen collateral damage can be prima facie permissible. I think that we can find a way of separating out those cases that intuitively are Terrorism and prima facie impermissible from those that we think are collateral damage and prima facie permissible.

Here, very briefly, is a suggestion on how to do this. Jointly sufficient grounds for the prima facie impermissibility of Terrorism (rather than some other act) might be given by (1) the presence in an agent of the intention to harm and terrorize Civilians, either as an end or means, against their interests and without their consent (necessary for an act to fall in the category of Terrorism), (2) the necessity, given the agent's act, of a causal (or end) role for harm and terror,[44] and (3) the absence of (i) any other effect of the agent's act, intended or not, that could justify the harm and terror and whose production does not require, given the agent's act, a causal (or end) role for the harm and terror, and (ii) any other wrong that the agent intends, whose production is both sufficient for the agent to act and does not require, given the agent's act, a causal (or end) role for the harm and terror.[45]

This is a new proposal, based on the cases of both permissible and impermissible bombing that we have discussed, to separate out factors distinctive of Terrorism that also make it prima facie impermissible. According to this proposal, it is factors (2) and (3) that have this joint role. The proposal differs from those that focus on intention to harm and terrorize or the actual causal route through harm and terror as the source of prima facie impermissibility. (However, intention to harm and terrorize are present to conceptually characterize the act as Terrorism.) It is different, in part, because of its focus on the necessity, given one's act, of a role (causal or end) for harm and terror. That is, it involves a modal condition.[46]

Cases that have been standardly used to illustrate terrorism and terror bombing in war have the characteristics that satisfy this proposal. For example, they involve a bombardier who drops bombs directly on children (or on empty territory near them). He intends the harm to them and the resulting terror as a means to an opponent's surrender. Further, no other aspect or effect of his act that does *not* require Civilian harm and terror as a means to produce it either justifies the deaths and terror as side effects or constitute some other wrong that is intended and that is sufficient for him to act. (This contrasts with the Baby Killer Nation bombardier discussed earlier.) It has been mistakenly thought that the intention to harm and terrorize or the actual (as opposed to necessary) causal route through harm and terror to a goal is the definitive characteristic for determining the presence of Terrorism and its impermissibility.[47]

But how will the proposal distinguish cases of impermissible Terrorism from the Munitions Grief Case (discussed in n. 15)? In that case, we will not bomb a military facility unless doing so does have a side effect of killing children, for if their parents are not grieving, they will quickly rebuild the facility. This means there is a necessary causal role for Civilian deaths, yet this does not make bombing impermissible. In the Munitions Grief Case, unlike Terrorism, the deaths are caused by, and help *sustain*, the very outcome (the facility destroyed) that could justify the Civilian deaths. There is, I believe, a distinction between harm and terror playing a necessary causal role by (i) *sustaining* a good rather than (ii) *producing* a good. It is also important whether the harm and terror that play this sustaining role are effects of the good we have already achieved without them. In sum, on my view, what causes the Civilian deaths and whether these deaths go on to "produce" a new effect or instead "sustain" one already produced can affect the permissibility of doing what causes the harm and terror.[48]

However, it may be asked, why should the necessity, given one's act, of harm and terror for producing an end (in conjunction with the absence of any other justifying effect) be a special factor bearing on the moral impermissibility of an act, by contrast to the necessity, given one's act, of harm and terror as a side effect of producing an end?[49] We still need a deeper explanation, but perhaps we now know what we need to explain. That is, let us suppose that the new proposal, unlike the DDE, does not pick out as impermissible any acts that we intuitively think are permissible (and vice versa). This is not enough to give a deep explanation for why the factor emphasized in this proposal plays a special role in rendering acts prima facie impermissible. We would still have to provide an explanation of why, for example, the necessity of a productive role for harm and terror (in conjunction with the other elements of the proposal) is a special mark against an act. It is not my goal in this chapter to provide such a deep explanation.[50] I do, however, believe that what I have called "purity in the causal chain necessary, given one's act, to produce some good" is an important part of morality. This implies (very approximately) that certain good effects cannot justify one's conduct if evil (whose existence is not already justified) is necessary, given one's act, to produce those good effects.[51]

III. *Permissible Terrorism?*

Let us assume (for the sake of argument) that there are special objections to terrorism (standard or nonstandard) that can rule it out even if collateral damage would be permissible (holding constant harm and terror). Now I wish to consider whether even acts that require harm and terror to produce a goal could sometimes ultimately be justified by producing that goal (in the absence of another effect of the act that could justify the harm and terror as side effects). If the acts could be so justified, some terrorism would be ultimately permissible, although prima facie impermissible. In order to decide whether this is possible, consider the following points.

A. SUPREME EMERGENCY

How important and of what kind is the ultimate goal of the terrorist, and is a terrorist act the only way to achieve that goal? These factors would have to be considered if one is a "threshold deontologist," who holds that means that are usually impermissible to produce a greater good can sometimes be permissible when the good is important enough, of the right type, and there is no other way to achieve it.

For example, John Rawls proposed that terror bombing by a state would have been permissible had Great Britain been alone against the Nazis in the Second World War and terror bombing of Civilians was the only way, and reasonably likely, to stop Nazi world domination.[52] This is known as the supreme emergency exception. I believe that had a non-state Resistance movement remained after Britain's defeat, it could permissibly have done the same sort of bombing to defeat Nazi world domination, even if the bombing would then have been an instance of Terrorism (i.e., not done by a state).

Now consider a supreme emergency case in which Terrorism (or state-run terrorism) is *not* the only way to achieve a sufficiently important goal. If the prohibition on terror-killing is not absolute but has a threshold, then it could be overridden because the cost of using an alternative means to the important goal is too great. For example, even Warren Quinn, who defends the DDE, only thinks of intended killings as requiring more to justify them than side-effect ones.[53] Hence, his view suggests that if we were going to do what would kill a million people as a side effect and could achieve the same result by terror-killing one person who would not otherwise have died (so as to terrorize another person who would not otherwise have been affected), then this might be permissible.

B. NONSUPREME EMERGENCY

Next, consider a nonsupreme emergency case, in which terrorism is also not the only means to achieve a sufficiently important good of the right type. In order to decide whether Terrorism is still permissible, we must consider the means that would or could be used instead of killing and terrorizing Civilians. For example, suppose that there are three ways to defeat an unjust enemy. One way involves bombing a munitions plant. To the east of the munitions plant is a park. Suppose that if that plant is struck (for militarily sound reasons in order to defeat an unjust enemy), then a thousand people in the park would be killed and more terrorized, as a side effect. A second way to defeat the enemy is to terror bomb a thousand different people to the west of the munitions plant. A third way is to terror bomb 100 different people to the north of the plant. (See Figure 1.)

Suppose that given the goal, it would be permissible to bomb the munitions plant despite the collateral death and terror to the east. It could still be impermissible to terror bomb either to the west or north, given that there are moral objections (which we have been investigating) to terror bombing that do not apply to causing collateral deaths. These objections could be significant enough that even causing 900 more deaths collaterally in the east cannot override them. (That is, even if one is a threshold deontologist, the ratio between deaths and terror due to terrorism and those due to collateral damage may not be high enough to override special objections to terrorism.) Hence, the only course of conduct that is permissible among the three options involves more Civilian deaths and terror than at least one of the other ways of defeating the enemy. This is consist-

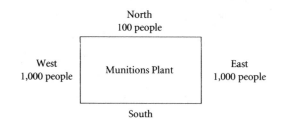

Figure 1

ent with a nonconsequentialist moral theory that claims that the right act is not always what produces the best consequences.

However, suppose that a fourth option becomes available: We can also defeat our enemy by directly terror bombing 100 of the very same people in the east who would die anyway collaterally if we bomb the munitions plant. I believe that terror bombing these people in the park instead of bombing the munitions plant would be permissible. This is so even if terror bombing 100 of the people in the park would have been wrong (in virtue of how the victims' deaths and terror were required as a means to produce a goal) if it were the only act that could have been performed. As a substitute for a permissible act of munitions bombing that would have caused the deaths of the same 100 people plus many more, what would be impermissible on its own becomes permissible *secondarily*. This is, in part, because those who die and are terrorized will be made no worse off than they otherwise would have permissibly been made, and the right not to be treated in the manner involved in terror bombing is weakened when the effects on one's life are no different from the effects of the act that would otherwise have permissibly been done. It is further grounds for the permissibility of terror bombing the 100 to the east that many others who would have died and been terrorized in collateral damage will be better off. This is an instance of what I have called the Principle of Secondary Permissibility (PSP).[54]

The 100 terror bombed in the east are unlike the 100 in the north, for if the people in the north were terror bombed, they would be made worse off than they otherwise would permissibly have been made. This is because if we do not terror bomb them, they could not have died as collateral damage at all and this would have been the only permissible way of causing their deaths. (This is on the assumption that there are moral objections to terror bombing that do not arise for collateral damage.) Hence, terror bombing them can be an impermissible alternative to bombing the munitions plant.

However, in discussing the PSP, we have moved away from the typical case of Terrorism, which involves killing and terrorizing people who would not suffer these fates soon anyway. We can reintroduce this factor by imagining a case almost like the one in which we terror bomb only some of those in the park who would have died and been terrorized collaterally. The one difference is that agents who are physically able to permissibly bomb the munitions plant cannot bring themselves to do so when they think it is their only option, because of the large amount of collateral harm and terror. Their refraining is supererogatory because it increases the risks of war to them. They then find out that they can achieve their aims as well by directly killing and terrorizing 100 of those thousand Civilians that they are still physically able to, but *will not*, permissibly kill and terrorize collaterally.[55] These 100 people would not die shortly anyway, but they would be alive only because agents supererogatorily refrain from doing what they still can permissibly do. Indeed, if only those 100 would die and be terrorized collaterally, the agents would *not* refrain from permissibly bombing the munitions plant. Due to these facts, I think it becomes permissible for the agents to harm and terrorize the smaller subset who would not have been killed soon anyway as a means to defeat the enemy. This is an extension of the PSP, so I call it the Extended Principle of Secondary Permissibility (EPSP).[56] (By contrast, the fact that people in the north would not soon die anyway is not due to agents supererogatorily refraining from doing a permissible act. This can affect whether people in the north are morally susceptible to being terror bombed when such bombing is otherwise impermissible.)

Surprisingly, the PSP and EPSP imply that those who have access to alternative permissible means with which to accomplish their goals may sometimes permissibly engage in terrorism when those who lack alternative means may not. They may do this because the terrorism is the alternative to permissibly producing even more death and terror to the very same people as well as to many others. (This is consistent with there being other reasons why those who lack alternative permissible means may sometimes permissibly use terrorism when those who do have alternative permissible means may not. For example, sometimes the alternative permissible means are less harmful than terrorism to a given set of people, so those who have alternative means must use them. But those who lack such permissible means could face a "supreme emergency" that justifies terror.)

Earlier, we said that using the Meaning Theory to categorize cases where appropriate military targets are hit by agents with terrorist intentions will yield the result that some Terrorist acts are permissible. On the basis of our present discussion, we can conclude that even if we reject the

Meaning Theory, we cannot say that particular Terrorist acts are impermissible until we know the number who will be similarly affected if another act is done, who those affected would be, and whether the alternative act was permissible. This is in addition to having to know whether a threshold on abiding by deontological constraints on Terrorism has been reached, even when it is not a substitute for some other act.

This examination of Terrorism shows, I think, that there may be no simple answer to the question of whether Standard or Nonstandard Terrorism is impermissible in general, although easy answers will certainly be available in particular cases. This implies that when Terrorism is impermissible, it is not because it is the sort of act that can never be permissible.

IV. *International Proposals*

Given how we have reasoned and our conclusions so far, we are in a position, I believe, to reflect on some proposals for dealing with terrorism (standard or nonstandard) offered by world leaders. It is true that I have used hypothetical cases in order to help make my points, and it may be said that public policy should not, or at least need not, be formulated to take account of hypothetical cases that are unlikely to occur. However, some of the statesmen who have formulated proposals for dealing with terrorism have themselves made use of hypothetical cases that seem unlikely to occur in dealing with related public policy issues. For example, some officials are reluctant to rule out torture because they consider so-called "ticking bomb" hypothetical cases affecting the lives of many people, when we are assumed to have perfect knowledge that we can stop the bomb if and only if we torture the terrorist who set the bomb in order to save his victims.[57] If they are right to consider such hypothetical cases in formulating public policy on torture, then it also may be right to consider the sort of hypotheticals I have been using in formulating public policy on terrorism.[58]

A. GLOBAL SUMMIT STATEMENT

So let us consider how what I have said bears on the recommendations about terrorism proposed in UN and global summit documents. Consider the global summit statement on terrorism (which I shall divide into two sections): "We (the world leaders) (1) affirm that the targeting and deliberate killing of civilians and noncombatants cannot be justified or legitimized by any cause or grievance, and (2) we declare that any action intended to cause death or serious bodily harm to civilians or noncombatants, when the purpose of such an act, by its nature or context, is to intimidate a population or to compel a government or an international organization to carry out or to abstain from any act, cannot be justified on any grounds, and constitutes an act of terrorism."[59]

A part of section 2 of this statement is concerned with merely conceptual matters. It tries to provide at least a partial definition of terrorism and refers to intentions to harm noncombatants with the further intention to intimidate a population or government in order to change their policies. Assuming the intimidation comes about by fear or terror, this coincides with what I have described as a characteristic of terrorism. However, I argued that the characterization in section 2 was not a sufficient condition for terrorism, even when combined with intentionally doing an act that actually kills and terrorizes. For imagine the case in which Baby Killer Nation, aiming to kill in order to terrorize and thereby to protest pronatalist policy, bombs the Nazi military WTC (or uses bombs that as a side effect bring down the WTC). It thereby brings about civilian deaths that, in the context, intimidate a population and (we assume) cause the government to change its policies. We assume that the Nazi WTC is a permissible object of direct attack given that its destruction would help end Nazi rule, and that such action would justify some side-effect deaths and terror. Baby Killer Nation's bombing the Nazi WTC (or using bombs that destroy it as a side effect) would not be terrorism, I think, at least if Baby Killer Nation makes acting on its intentions contingent on there being a military facility to destroy and there is no time it can hit that facility when civilians will not be harmed. Furthermore, I have argued that if the act of destroying the military site would be permissible, even taking into account the further collateral damage, when done by a party lacking Baby Killer Nation's bad intentions, it will remain so when Baby Killer Nation does it. Hence, the definition in section 2 could be improved by taking account of the fact that although an agent may intend harm and terror to Civilians in order to change government policies, other aspects of its act can make its act not be terrorism and even be permissible. (I shall suggest such an improvement after considering other problems with the statement.[60])

Other parts of the statement are concerned with moral conclusions. Section 1 of the summit declaration claims that a part of terrorism, namely, targeting and deliberate killing of Civilians, cannot be justified by any cause. Section 2 claims that any action intended to cause death to Civilians with the further characteristics that make this terrorism cannot be justified by any cause. Suppose we separate out the intention to kill Civilians from the behavior to which it leads. Is it true that this intention (independent of the overt act) cannot ever be justified? Above, I described types of cases in which, I suggested, such an intention could be justified. First, there was the hypothetical supreme emergency case in which the Resistance in a defeated Britain intended to kill Civilians as this was the only way that had a reasonable chance of stopping Nazi worldwide domination. Second, it seems permissible to intend to kill a small subset of the Civilians whom one would (or can) permissibly kill as collateral damage, especially when one foresees that the collateral damage would anyway intimidate people and lead to a change in government policy.

Now suppose we consider the overt acts that are prompted by the intentions in question, not just the intentions themselves. In the two cases just mentioned, the acts as well as the intentions are justified. By contrast, Baby Killer Nation's intentions, per se, are not justified. However, when Baby Killer Nation bombs any military facility causing harm to people that would be justified as collateral damage, then its action will be justified even though the intention in acting is not justified.

Notice that the fact that an agent in the Baby Killer Cases targets the military WTC does *not* mean that he is *not* doing this in order to deliberately kill Civilians. Sometimes it is possible to fulfill the aim of killing or terrorizing someone only indirectly, by hitting another target that will cause people harm. I think that doing this also constitutes targeting those Civilians for harm. However, "targeting and deliberate killing" in section 1 of the statement may suggest something narrower, when there is no intermediate target whose being hit is a means to harming Civilians. The phrase may be meant to apply only to cases in which Civilians are directly attacked. (I shall call this Direct Targeting.)[61] If this were all the statement intended to rule out, it would be too narrow, both morally and as a conception of terrorism. Furthermore, even such Direct Targeting could sometimes be justified. For example, it seems permissible to directly bomb a small subset of the Civilians whom one would (or can) otherwise permissibly kill as collateral damage, in order to reduce total numbers harmed.

If it would be better to formulate a public policy that is not subject to such counterexamples, policymakers could make changes that would make the summit proposal more accurate. While a philosopher might be helpful in locating problems that need to be fixed, she may not be the best person to construct easily understandable language for such a modified proposal. Nevertheless, I shall make a suggestion that points to where improvements would help (even if the result is not perfectly correct or ideal for public policy purposes):

> We affirm that the targeting and deliberate killing of civilians and noncombatants cannot be justified or legitimized except when necessary in supreme emergencies, or also in nonsupreme emergencies (i) when it is not further against the interests (that may already, in some other way, be permissibly set back) of the very people to be targeted and killed, or (ii) when other aspects or effects of the act make it permissible despite the harm and terror it causes. We also declare that any action intended to cause death or serious bodily harm to civilians or noncombatants, when the purpose of such an act, by its nature or context, is to intimidate a population or to compel a government or international organization to carry out or to abstain from any act, constitutes an act of terrorism and cannot be justified, unless other aspects or effects of the act make it be not terrorist and/or permissible despite the harm and terror it causes, or else the conditions of supreme emergency or not being further against the interests (that may already, in some other way, be permissibly set back) of those harmed are satisfied.[62]

Alternatively, the proposal could be modified so as to avoid referring to some intentions in the following way:

> We affirm that acts that require the killing of civilians and noncombatants as ends or means to a goal cannot be justified or legitimized,

except if necessary in supreme emergencies or also in nonsupreme emergencies (i) when this is not further against the interests (that may already, in some other way, be permissibly set back) of the very people to be targeted and killed, or (ii) when other aspects or effects of the act make it be permissible despite the harm and terror it causes. We also declare that any action requiring death or serious bodily harm to civilians or noncombatants in order to intimidate a population or to compel a government or international organization to carry out or to abstain from any act, both constitutes an act of terrorism and cannot be justified, unless other aspects or effects of the act make it be not terrorist and/or permissible, or else the conditions of supreme emergency or not further against the interests (that may already, in some other way, be permissibly set back) of those harmed are satisfied.

B. DRAFT CONVENTION

A very differently worded proposal (that is described as a definition) is included in the Draft Convention on International Terrorism. There, terrorism is defined as:

> ...a person's unlawfully and intentionally causing or threatening to cause violence by means of firearms, weapons, explosives, any lethal devices or dangerous substances, which results, or is likely to result, in death or serious bodily injury to a person, a group of persons or serious damage to property—whether for public use, a State or Government facility, a public transportation system or an infrastructure facility. Acts of terrorism also include such a person's attempt to commit such an offense....The Draft Convention requires the Parties to establish as criminal offenses under its domestic laws the aforementioned offenses, which are of such a nature as to create terror, fear, or insecurity... such offense shall be under no circumstances justifiable by considerations of a political, philosophical, ideological, racial, ethnic, religious, or other similar nature. (From "UN Draft Comprehensive Convention on International Terrorism" [as of July 2004].)

This proposed definition has its own particular problems (in addition to some it shares with the summit proposal discussed above). It assumes that terrorism involves causing or threatening to cause an unlawful act of intentional violence. This leaves it open that there are lawful acts of intentional violence. However, it rules out, by definition, that these lawful acts could be terrorism in virtue of having all properties that other acts of illegal terrorism have *except illegality*. Intuitively, however, it seems that we could sometimes recognize that intentionally blowing up civilians in a marketplace is terrorism before we knew whether it was illegal or legal (as a result, perhaps, of a court order permitting it to be done in a supreme emergency). Furthermore, the definition speaks of intentionally causing violence that results in serious harm to persons or serious damage to property, but it does not distinguish between noncombatant and combatant persons or between military and civilian property. Perhaps this is because it assumes that deliberate violence that harms combatants and military property is sometimes not unlawful, and it is only concerned with what are always unlawful acts. Alternatively, it is assuming the absence of circumstances of war and so attacks on noncivilians, who will then be noncombatants, are just as much terrorism as attacks on civilians. (This is suggested by the fact that the document says that terrorism is to be ruled out as a criminal offense, not as a violation of the laws of war.)

Furthermore, in speaking of intentionally causing violence using devices that are "likely to result in death" and "which are of such a nature as to create terror," the definition does not distinguish between (a) intentionally causing violence that results in death and terror as collateral damage and either (b) intentionally causing violence intending death and terror, or (c) intentionally causing violence that causes death and terror as a required means (perhaps unintended) to produce one's end. The definition's not making these distinctions is problematic unless it is being assumed that intentionally doing what causes serious collateral damage is sometimes not unlawful and the definition is only concerned with what are always unlawful acts.

One of the biggest problems with the proposal is that it seems to imply that illegal intentional violence that can result in serious harm or damage and is of such a nature as to create terror, fear, or insecurity is always terrorism. However, many common criminal acts have these properties, yet they are not terrorism.

The draft convention also claims that terrorism is never justifiable for political purposes. It would then have ruled out a British resistance movement during Nazi worldwide domination intentionally causing harm to civilians if this had been necessary and sufficient to overturn Nazi worldwide domination. Yet such resistance seems morally permissible in a supreme emergency. Other things equal, it would be better to formulate a proposal that rules out only impermissible terrorism.

Notes

1. This chapter is a revised version of "Terrorism and Intending Evil," published in *Philosophy & Public Affairs* 36 (2008): 157–86. The substance of that article was given as the 2007 Oslo Lecture on Moral Philosophy at the University of Oslo. Sections I through IV are based on, follow in structure, and make use of material in, but revise and add to, parts of my "Terrorism and Several Moral Distinctions," *Legal Theory* 12 (Spring 2006): 19–69. I am grateful for comments to Rudiger Bittner, Derek Parfit, Thomas Pogge, Wlodek Rabinowicz, Julian Savulescu, Geoffrey Sayer-McCord, Suzanne Uniacke, members of the conference on moral philosophy held in Brugges, Belgium, June 2007, and to the editors of *Philosophy & Public Affairs*. I am also grateful for comments from audiences at the University of Calgary, Fall 2005, at the Plenary Session of the Australasian Philosophical Association, Canberra, July 2006, at the University of Oslo, August 30, 2007, at the Conference on War in the 21st Century, Jean Beer Blumenfeld Center for Ethics, Georgia State University, October 2007, at the Law School, University of Texas (Austin), September 2008, and at the Uehiro Lectures, Oxford University, November 2008.

2. Some noncivilian military personnel may be noncombatants too (when there is no ongoing war, for example). I discussed terrorism against combatants in my "Failures of Just War Theory," *Ethics* 114 (July 2004): 650–92.

3. Interestingly, this characterization of Terrorism seems to apply to some of the plagues that the God of the Old Testament sent on ancient Egyptians, e.g., the intentional killing of first-born sons as a means of altering Pharaoh's policies. (If the God of the Old Testament is considered the legitimate ruler of the world, then His acts may be more like state-sponsored terrorism than like Terrorism. I owe this last point to Noam Zohar.) Jeremy Waldron, in his

"Terrorism and the Uses of Terror," *The Journal of Ethics* 8 (2004): 5–35, discusses various aims of the terrorist.

4. Prima facie wrong and pro tanto wrong are distinguished (roughly) in the following way: An act is prima facie wrong, although ultimately justified, when factors that would make the act wrong get completely cancelled out in particular circumstances. An act is pro tanto wrong, although ultimately justified, when wrong-making factors remain present but are overridden by other factors.

5. I shall use "killing" to also include "grave injury."

6. For more discussion of the distinction between simply doing something to a person (such as killing him) and doing something to a person in order to get him to do something (coercively), see Chapter 1 above.

7. It is true that we might tolerate a few murders occurring in a society rather than shift money to increased police protection and away from providing small goods (such as zoos) to each of many other people. This is consistent with its being a greater wrong for someone to murder a person than to eliminate a small good to each of many people. It is also possible that if a harm less than death is almost as bad (e.g., total paralysis and locked-in syndrome), the aggregate of lesser losses to many might outweigh a greater loss suffered by each of a few. When it is morally appropriate to aggregate is a controversial issue. See my *Morality, Mortality, Vol.* 1 (New York: Oxford University Press, 1993), and *Intricate Ethics* (New York: Oxford University Press, 2007), ch. 2, for some discussion of this issue in connection with allocation of scarce resources. See also "Terrorism and Several Moral Distinctions."

8. I have discussed this issue further in "Terrorism and Several Moral Distinctions," and "Types of Terror Bombing and Shifting Responsibility," in *Action, Ethics, and Responsibility*, eds. J. K. Campbell, M. O'Rourke, and H. Silverstein (Cambridge, MA: MIT Press, 2010); and in Chapter 1 above.

9. I drew this distinction between types of terror in "Terrorism and Several Moral Distinctions," characterizing the first understanding as "nonmechanical" and the second as "mechanical." Jeremy Waldron, in his "Terrorism and the Uses of Terror" (which I read only subsequent to writing "Terrorism and Several Moral Distinctions"), drew a similar distinction. What he referred to as "Arendtian" fear corresponds to what I called "mechanical" fear, and what he referred to as "Jack Benny" fear corresponds to what I called "nonmechanical" fear. In Arendtian fear, one is in an unreasoning panic; in Jack Benny fear, a threat leads one to weigh the costs and benefits of giving in.

10. This is emphasized by Samuel Scheffler in his "Is Terrorism Morally Distinctive," *Journal of Political Philosophy* 14(1) (2006): 1–17.

11. For more detailed discussion of this issue, see "Terrorism and Several Moral Distinctions."

12. By "liable" I here mean to imply that someone would have no complaint if something is done to him on account of what he has done. Liability is distinct from desert, as someone can be liable to be harmed even if he does not deserve to be harmed. I take desert to imply that it is a positively good feature of a states of affairs if someone gets what he deserves; this need not be so if someone gets that to which he is liable. Someone need not be liable to harm in order for it to be permissible to harm him, as it could be permissible to engage in an activity that harms someone when the person harmed retains a right to complain and may be entitled to compensation. For distinctions along these lines see Jeff McMahan's *Killing in War* (Oxford: Clarendon Press, 2009).

13. This is like a case discussed by Judith Jarvis Thomson in "Self-Defense," *Philosophy & Public Affairs* 20 (1991): 283–310.

14. It may be asked why I imagine the WTC, in particular, as a purely military target in the hypothetical case, rather than just imagine a terrorist attacking an ordinary military base. One of my purposes in this discussion is ultimately to draw implications for the actual attack on the WTC on September 11, 2001 (9/11). I think that the best route to this is by imagining hypothetical variations on that case (which rightly disturbs and draws the attention of many people). Perhaps it is the best route because imagining these variations makes us think more analytically about the actual case.

15. It is important to see that this may not necessarily exclude bombing some military facility *only because* Civilians will be killed. That is, there is a conceptual difference between intending to kill Civilians and acting only because we will kill them. Consider what I call the Munitions Grief Case discussed in *Morality, Mortality, Vol. 2* (New York: Oxford University Press, 1996) and *Intricate Ethics*. During a just war, we need to bomb a munitions plant for military purposes and know this will cause collateral deaths of children next door. Their deaths would be proportionate if the destruction of the plant were permanent. However, the community would quickly rebuild it better than ever—thus making bombing pointless and the collateral damage disproportionate—if not for the fact that they will be depressed by the death of their children. Hence, it is only because (we know) the children will die that we bomb the munitions plant; we would

not bomb if they did not die. I think bombing in this case is permissible and not inconsistent with the DDE, even though we would act because the deaths help sustain the destruction of the plant. We here take advantage of an unavoidable side effect of bombing the plant; we do nothing extra that is not necessary to bomb the munitions plant merely in order that the bombing does cause the collateral damage.

This case helps show, I think, that we can distinguish conceptually among effects that are intended, merely foreseen, or because of which we act. I have referred to a view that takes account of these three distinctions as the Doctrine of Triple Effect (DTE). See *Intricate Ethics*, ch. 4.

16. Notice that in the Munitions Grief Case, the harm and terror do have a causal role (even a required causal role) in bringing about goals. If bombing in the Munitions Grief Case is permissible, the causal roles interpretation of the DDE is either wrong or must be modified. We will discuss this issue below.

17. I have tried to deal with this issue in "Justifications for Killing Noncombatants in War," *Midwest Studies in Philosophy* 24 (2000): 219–28; in "Failures of Just War Theory", in my *Intricate Ethics*, ch. 5, and in "Some Moral Issues about Killing in War," *Oxford Handbook on Death* (New York: Oxford University Press, forthcoming).

18. I shall assume the Nazis control only the United States (or even just part of it), and they present no threat of world domination. I do this to interfere with conceiving of the case as what is called a "supreme emergency." Supreme emergencies are sometimes thought to allow us to override ordinary moral constraints. I discuss a supreme emergency case in Section IV.

19. It is my desire to discuss uncontroversially innocent victims and bad agents that leads me to conceive of Baby Killer Nation and the Nazis.

20. In earlier work on this subject, I used the term "cover" rather than "pretext." But I am concerned to convey the idea that Baby Killer Nation behaves as the Resistance would, not that it is necessarily trying to conceal its intentions for its behavior. The term "cover" seemed to suggest the latter to an editor of *Philosophy & Public Affairs* in an earlier version of this chapter, and this prompted the change in language. With respect to the question of whether an agent's intention affects the permissibility of his act, whether the agent tries to conceal his intentions is beside the point. Intentions with which acts are done are often important because they are predictive of an agent's other behavior. That is, people with bad intentions may act differently in changed circumstances from people without those intentions, even when they act in

the same way in some circumstances. For example, suppose that bombing the military facility in the WTC caused no side-effect harm to people. The Resistance would continue its efforts to bomb, but Baby Killer Nation would not. However, this does not show that when the overt acts and effects are the same for the well-intentioned and nonwell-intentioned agent, the latter's overt acts are impermissible. Yet this is what the DDE claims is true. In order to test the DDE, I will suppose throughout this discussion that different intentions never show up in different behavior, so all behavior and effects will be the same; only the intentions differ.

21. While I think Baby Killer's action is permissible, it is not because it is permissible that I conclude it is not Terrorism, as I have been leaving it open that Terrorism might sometimes be permissible.

22. I discuss the Bad Man Trolley Case in *Intricate Ethics*, ch. 5. I discuss the distinction between acting with the intention (or in order) to cause *x* and acting because (or on condition) that one causes *x* in *Intricate Ethics*, ch. 4, among other places. See also Chapter 3 in this volume.

23. I believe that sometimes the same is true when an agent produces a greater good even if he would not condition his harming someone on his producing the greater good. For more on this, see "Terrorism and Several Moral Distinctions."

24. Similarly, in the Bad Man Trolley Case, as presented so far, the bad man intends to turn the trolley away from the five (albeit as a means to killing his enemy). It may be thought that intending to turn the trolley from the five is good or appropriate, and this explains why his act is not murder. However, we can also construct a variation on the Bad Man Trolley Case in which the bad man does not intend to turn the trolley away from the five; this is a mere side effect of something else that he intends to do in order to kill his enemy. For example, he intends to press a switch that will send an electric current into his enemy on the side track. Pressing this switch is also the only thing that will turn the trolley away from the five but the trolley that is turned away from the five plays no role in killing his enemy, as it is redirected onto another side track. We can imagine that it is only on condition that pressing the switch has the side effect of turning the trolley from the five that the bad man will press it. This is because he seeks to do something that would be permissible for a good person to do, as a pretext for killing his enemy. Notice that there are some who would argue that it is impermissible, even to save the five, to do what kills the man on the side track when his death is not an effect of the trolley turning away from the five. In particular, it is impermissible when the death is the effect of a mere means

(pressing the switch) to turning the trolley away from the five. (I discuss this view in Chapter 5 of *Intricate Ethics*). However, those who believe that collateral damage can be permissible even when it is caused by a mere means to a greater good, such as an exploding bomb, cannot raise this objection. (In particular, the DDE does not rule out proportionate harm being caused by necessary means to the greater good.) If pressing the switch would be permissible for those trying to save the five, then in this second Bad Man Trolley Case as well, I do not think that the bad man's intention implies that he commits murder.

25. As I here use "means," it involves what an agent does that brings about a goal of his, regardless of whether he intends the means.

26. Again, this is like a case discussed by Thomson in "Self-Defense."

27. Even if they do not know this but it is true, their act may not be Terrorism.

28. See his "Intention and Permissibility," *Proceedings of the Aristotelian Society* (2000), where he offers his own explanation of Judith Jarvis Thomson's view that intention does not affect the permissibility of acts of bombing in wartime, as proposed in her "Self-Defense." See also his *Moral Dimensions* (Cambridge, MA: Harvard University Press, 2008), ch 1. He does not claim intention never affects permissibility.

29. Again, I note that an agent's acting on condition that some good occur may not be necessary for permissibility. However, his constraining himself in this way may have additional significance, beyond others having no right to object to his act. See Chapter 3 on this.

30. It is interesting (and nonutilitarian) that it is morally preferable that an agent who will not be happy do the bombing. I owe this point to David Lyons.

31. I discuss the "unintended good" objection to the DDE further in my *Intricate Ethics*, ch. 4 (among other places). It might be suggested that one can tell if collateral damage is morally justified only if one knows an agent's purpose in attacking a military target. (Some say this is how the laws of war deal with collateral damage.) On this view, collateral damage caused by the Resistance could be justified, given that its goal is ending Nazi military power, but not collateral damage (let alone targeted harm) caused by Baby Killer Nation when it does not intend to get rid of the Nazis. What I have argued suggests that the purposes of a group are less important and we should look to what it effects to see if the collateral damage is justified. The Nazis should be gotten rid of, regardless of whether Baby Killer Nation agrees, and getting rid of them is enough to justify the collateral damage (assuming that anything can justify the collateral damage). This issue also arises when we consider reasons for starting war between nation states. See Chapter 3 below.

32. I shall expand on this explanation below in Section G.
33. Thomas Scanlon argues that intentions are relevant to the meaning of actions, even if not to their permissibility. See his *Moral Dimensions*, ch. 2.
34. There may be other views besides the Meaning Theory, according to which what is done in P(i) and P(ii) are Terrorism. My conclusion will hold for these views, too.
35. This conclusion differs from the one I drew in "Terrorism and Several Moral Distinctions."
36. I discuss such cases in *Intricate Ethics*, ch. 5.
37. Thomas Nagel, "War and Massacre," *Philosophy & Public Affairs* 1 (Winter 1972): 123–44.
38. In his *Moral Dimensions*, Scanlon emphasizes that he is not concerned at this point in his discussion to defend the principles concerning prohibition on use of deadly force or exceptions to it. He is only concerned to show that they need not be explained in terms of intentions.
39. I described such cases in "Terrorism and Several Moral Distinctions."
40. The permissibility of deliberately harming Civilians for military purposes would not eliminate all distinctions between treatment of combatants and Civilians, as we might still be required to harm combatants before harming Civilians or require that more good be done in order to justify harming Civilians than combatants.
41. To my surprise, it seems that many do not consider cases like these to be terrorism at all, simply because military advantage is at issue. Furthermore, if comparable acts were carried out in a declared war by a nation-state, some do not think causing such harm and terror to Civilians is terror bombing or forbidden. This is because the acts are part of a military mission not intended to merely change political policies or affect outcomes only through pressure on political processes. Apparently, such intentional harm and terror for military purposes was used on Civilians in the Second World War. Professor John Lewis, a historian of war, confirmed this [in conversation]. He too seemed surprised that such use of harm and terror could be ruled impermissible on the same grounds as Terrorism or the standard form of terror bombing in war between nation-states, which seeks to end a war by demoralizing Civilians. I discuss this issue in "Types of Terror Bombing and Shifting Responsibility," in *Action, Ethics, and Responsibility*, eds. J. K. Campbell, M. O'Rourke, and H. Silverstein (Cambridge, MA: MIT Press, 2010).

42. *Moral Dimensions*, p. 32.

43. When we respond to the threat combatants present by eliminating that threat, this is referred to as eliminative agency. When we use either combatants or Civilians, not to eliminate their threat but for other advantage (even military advantage), this is referred to as opportunistic agency. These terms were introduced by Warren Quinn in "Action, Intentions, and Consequences: The Doctrine of Double Effect," presented in his *Morality and Action* (New York: Cambridge University Press, 1993), pp. 175–93. See also my discussion in Chapter 1.

44 Notice that harm and terror could be necessary to produce some goal given an agent's act, even if it is not necessary tout court (because there are other acts he could have done that would not require harm and terror to achieve his goal). The fact that there are other acts he could have done that would not require harm and terror to produce a goal does not rule out that an act that he actually does requires harm and terror to produce the goal.

45. The addition of (ii) contrasts with the proposal in "Terrorism and Several Moral Distinctions."

46. For more on the theoretical background for this proposal, see my *Intricate Ethics*, ch. 5. I there discuss the role of a modal component (e.g., the necessity, given one's act, of a certain causal route to produce a goal) in an account of permissible and impermissible acts. I also distinguish producing a goal from sustaining it.

47. I have discussed (in *Intricate Ethics*) another approach to distinguishing Terrorism from collateral damage to Civilians that focuses not on actual intentions of agents but on the sort of intentions someone could reasonably have given the facts in a case. Suppose that there is some aspect or effect of one's act besides the harm and terror it causes that could justify the harm and terror as side effects. Then some agent, even if not this one, could intend, and do the act for the sake of, whatever aspect justifies the harm and terror. If such an agent could justifiably do the act, then (it may be said) even an agent with the wrong intention may permissibly do it. However, in cases where harm and terror are necessary, given one's act, to produce either the desired outcome or a different, potentially justifying, outcome, no agent (it might be said) could reasonably do the act without intending the harm and terror. Hence, the act becomes prima facie wrong for the current agent. This is a modal condition applied to intentions: we ask whether it is possible that a reasonable agent do this act without intending harm and terror, or whether it is necessary that a reasonable agent

do this act with such an intention. This alternative approach is not correct, I believe. First, it gets things backward. For we know that an act could not give an agent lacking an intention to cause harm and terror a reason to do it by looking at the act's properties independent of the agent's intentions. It is these properties that drive the speculation about possible nonwrongful intentions (or wrongful intentions not involving harm and terror) for doing the act. So why not rest with the presence or absence of these properties as grounds for permissibility or impermissibility? The alternative approach is also problematic because, I believe, a rational agent need not always intend whatever is necessary to produce his goal since he may know he will bring it about without intending it. Yet an act may be impermissible because it requires an agent to cause harm and terror, even if he need not intend these to produce his end. (I discuss this issue in Chapter 4 of *Intricate Ethics*, and aspects of it in Chapter 3 of this volume, among other places.)

48. For more on this, see *Intricate Ethics*, ch. 5.

49. The necessity of producing Civilian harm and terror as an end in itself is clearly wrong. This is because it is bad in itself and, by hypothesis in the cases we are now discussing, there is no effect that justifies it.

50. Some things that Thomas Scanlon says in his *Moral Dimensions* may seem to suggest an answer. Scanlon considers a nonwar case involving a person B, whose presence at a conference would be useful to person A (pp. 112–15). He argues that it could be impermissible for A to withhold information from B about the useful effect his presence would have, at least if he invites B to the conference. He claims (p. 113), "We have reason to care about what ends we will be promoting in choosing certain action and therefore reason to want to know what those are before deciding how to act." B may, after all, be opposed to having a good effect on A for understandable reasons. Scanlon argues that it is not A's intention in "using" B for the good effect he will have that triggers the requirement that B be informed and give consent to go to the conference. For, he says (p. 114), if A *did not intend* for B to come to the conference but knows that B will come, he also should inform B of the effect it will have on A, if he comes.

This discussion might seem to apply to the contrast of terror bombing and collateral damage in the following way: We may not terror bomb because people may object to the effect that harm and terror to them will have, or they may object to having a causal role in the production of an effect, even if they do not object to the effect per se. Hence, we would need consent if they had a causal role, but would not need it if the same harm and terror were a mere side effect as in collateral damage.

There seem to be several problems with this proposal. First, in the case Scanlon discusses, B's presence has a *necessary* causal role in producing the good effect on A. However, there might be cases where B *in fact* has a causal role in producing the effect, though if he had not shown up at the conference, the same effect would have come about by another route. Suppose that A's informing B of her causal role would interfere with the other path to A's success (not through B). Would Scanlon think it impermissible for A not to inform B of the actual causal role she will have? If so, this might create a problem for his view that it is permissible to bomb a military facility as a way to win a war, even when collateral damage will frighten citizens and it is this fear that actually helps end the war (as in the case I discuss on pp. 84–5). A second problem for this proposal may arise if those who would be terror bombed approve of the effect harm to them would have. For example, they may approve of the destruction of a military facility and would be happy to have a causal role in bringing it down, if it did not involve their death and terror. So their only objection to their role is their death and terror, and this is the same factor that is present when they die or are terrorized as collateral damage. It seems that even in a case of terror bombing where people do not object to having a causal role per se, it is still impermissible to cause the harm and terror to which they do object.

51. For more on this, see *Intricate Ethics*.
52. John Rawls, "Fifty Years after Hiroshima," *Dissent* (1995): 323–7. He did not think the actual terror bombing by Great Britain was permissible.
53. See his "Actions, Intentions, and Consequences: The Doctrine of Double Effect," *Philosophy & Public Affairs* 18 (1989): 334–51.
54. It is discussed in my *Morality, Mortality, Vol.* 2 and in *Intricate Ethics*.
55. I emphasize that this is a different case from one in which an agent could have permissibly caused the same collateral harm and terror *only* in the past but did not.
56. For more on this, see my *Intricate Ethics* and "Failures of Just War Theory."
57. For discussion of such cases, as well as ones that raise the question of whether torture is permissible even when the lives of many people are not at stake, see *Intricate Ethics*, ch. 8, and Chapter 1 in this book.
58. Of course, it is possible that these officials are wrong to use the unlikely hypotheticals to formulate policy on torture, and that public policy on both torture and terrorism should be based on likely scenarios, keeping in mind the likely consequences of a policy rather than its claim to philosophical

truth. These are complex issues in formulating public policy that I do not pretend to resolve here.

59. From draft of Millennium Summit, as reported in "UN Member States Struggle to Define Terrorism," by Thalif Deen, July 25, 2005, to be found at www.globalpolicy.org/empire/terrorwar/un/2005/0725define.htm.

60. A further problem with the conceptual part of section 2 is that it may not cover what I have called Nonstandard Terrorism. These could be cases where terror but not harm is intended and caused to Civilians, as in the Trees Case (p. 76). Or cases, such as the Stampede Case (p. 93), where terror and/or harm to Civilians is used not to change policies by intimidation but to subvert military operations, thereby leading to military defeat. I shall ignore this noninclusiveness of section 2 at this point.

61. It seems to correspond in one way to Nagel's notion of "doing something to" Civilians. See the discussion in Section III(E).

62. Understanding this modified proposal (and the other one further in the text) obviously depends on understanding the point of cases such as those involving the Nazi military WTC. In such a case, although Baby Killer Nation intends and requires death in order to achieve its own personal aims, there are other effects of its act and the way these can be produced that make its act not be terrorist (except on the Meaning Theory) and even make it be permissible.

REASONS FOR STARTING WAR: GOALS, CONDITIONS, AND PROPORTIONALITY

According to that part of just war theory known as *jus ad bellum*, among the conditions that must be met in order for it to be morally permissible to start a war are undertaking the war for a right reason and proportionality of relevant evils produced by the war to the relevant goods that are to be achieved by it.[1] In this chapter, I shall consider some aspects of these two conditions.

I. *Right Reasons or Not*

A. GOALS AND CONDITIONS FOR STARTING WAR

A right reason for beginning a war is taken to refer to starting the war with the intention to achieve (that is, for the sake of achieving) a limited set of goals, called a just cause, that would justify starting a war.[2] Among these limited goals, according to standard just war theory, are defense against physical aggression or attacks on sovereignty (even when it is only imminent). Prevention and cessation of genocide have been added as factors justifying armed intervention, though this may not strictly be referred to as war. (A right reason is not to be understood, I believe, as one's motive for having an intention. For example, one could have the aim of stopping aggression from various motives, including concern for world peace or hatred of the aggressor.)

I think that the "right reason" condition (so understood) on starting a war is incorrect if it is taken to have nonconsequentialist (or deontological) significance in itself, rather than as an indicator of possible good or bad consequences. That is, the intention to act for the sake of a factor that could constitute a just cause is, in itself, unnecessary from a deontological perspective in order for starting a war to be morally *permissible*, at the very least, if the factor that could be a just cause is or will be present regardless of one's intention, one knows this, and one acts on condition that the factor is or will be present.[3] By "acting on condition," I mean that if and only if one knows that the factor is or will be present (including will be caused by one's act), will one act. Acting for a right reason (as described above) might, however, have moral significance because even if it is not necessary in itself for permissibility, an agent's acting for a wrong reason may be a cause or sign of possible further bad consequences that others should take into account in deciding whether that agent's starting a war is permissible. (Those who are not consequentialists only deny that rightness is completely a function of consequences; they need not deny that consequences can sometimes help determine permissibility of action. Hence, even for nonconsequentialists the expected consequences of agent's acting for bad reasons could be morally relevant to permissibility.)

In this section, I shall first simply present cases in order to elicit intuitive judgments. I shall then try to clarify the conceptual distinction that I think exists between intending and acting on condition of an effect. Finally, I shall briefly consider how one might account for the moral insignificance of intention in our cases.

Consider a purely hypothetical example: Suppose it is permissible for some country—call it Weden—to begin a war against Germany to stop its invasion of Norway and also its genocide of Norwegians. However, neither Weden nor any other country is interested in starting a war for these purposes, but Weden knows that if it does stop the aggression and genocide, Norway will favor Weden in the sale of its oil resources. Getting such resources is not an aim that could justify Weden in starting a war, but that it will get resources is also not a reason against starting a war that stops aggression and genocide. Suppose Weden intervenes and stops aggression and genocide, but it does so only in order to get access to the resources that Norway will grant it, and it would not have intervened if it had not had this aim. Call this the Weden Oil Case. Despite the fact that its intention, necessary for it to act, is to get resources, it would still be permissible for it to go to war when this will stop the aggression and genocide. At the very least, if the factors that would justify the war—ending aggression and genocide—would come about, Weden knows they will, and acts on condition that they will, Weden's intervention can be permissible, I believe. (This is on the assumption that there are no other unacceptable effects of its action that would rule out war.)

The aim that is necessary to get an agent to start war *does* bear on the moral worth of its act. It also reveals the character of the agent who intervenes. As such, Weden may be entitled to no gratitude for its intervention in the Weden Oil Case. Also, often an agent's ultimate aim is a *sign* that besides stopping aggression and genocide, it might do other *im*permissible things that an agent who aimed only to stop aggression and genocide would not do. If having the intention to get resources would lead Weden to do impermissible acts, or is even a sign of some other fact about Weden that would lead it to do impermissible acts, it could be wrong for it to start war.[4] This would not be because of its aim to get resources per se, however, but because of the further, impermissible acts the country would commit. Focusing on the further impermissible acts that would ensue is using the consequences of its acting for some reason as a ground for determining that its starting war is impermissible. Of course, the further impermissible acts might have to be very grave in order that their occurrence justify not doing what will stop aggression and genocide.

Notice that in the Weden Oil Case, there are at least two ways in which the aggression and genocide could end. One way is that Weden aims to stop them as a means to getting the oil resources. For example, in Weden Oil Variant 1, Weden aims at ending aggression and genocide in order to make it possible for the formerly victimized Norwegians to reacquire power in the country and grant Weden access to oil. It might be thought that its aiming at ending aggression and genocide, even if just as a means to its ultimate aim of getting oil, makes its starting war permissible. I do not think this is true. For there is another way in which the aggression and genocide could be stopped that does not involve Weden's intending to stop them. Consider Weden Oil Variant 2: Suppose that ending aggression and genocide is a side effect of Weden's troops attacking the Germans who currently control the Norwegian oil resources and refuse to sell them to Weden. Weden attacks the German-controlled oil facilities in order to directly get control over the oil resources. However, it foresees that a side effect of Germany's losing control of oil is that its aggression and genocidal activity will also stop, and this is, in fact, the only way for these to stop. They foresee that if the Norwegians retake control of their oil, they will sell it to Weden.

In Variant 2, the fact that Weden does not aim to stop aggression and genocide even as a means to its goal of oil, and the fact that the goal that is necessary for it to start war could not itself justify starting a war, do not make its starting war impermissible, I believe. This is true, at the very least, when aggression and genocide's ending—which are factors that could be a just cause for war—will occur, Weden knows it will occur, and it conditions its intervention to get oil on the prospect of aggression and genocide ending. (It is assumed that no other effects that occur are sufficient reasons against Weden's intervention.)

Some may distinguish between acting with an intention that would not justify starting war and acting with a *bad* intention. They may agree that Weden's seeking oil does not make impermissible starting a war that stops aggression and genocide, because seeking oil is not a bad intention, even if it could not be a just cause for starting war. However, they would claim that Weden's acting with a *bad* intention can make its starting war impermissible.[5] In general, proponents of the Doctrine of Double Effect (DDE) will believe that intending evil makes an act impermissible. To consider a purely hypothetical case involving a bad intention, imagine Weden Oil Variant 3, in which Weden would intervene foreseeing that it would get oil and stop aggression and genocide, but with the bad intention of killing some civilians. That is, Weden foresees that waging war, no matter how carefully carried out, will kill a few civilians as side effects of attacks on military targets, and it intervenes in order to be able to kill these civilians. It would not do so unless its acts also end aggression and genocide, so this is a condition of its starting war. Furthermore, it would not kill civilians in any other manner or to any greater degree than would an agent who attacked the military facilities simply in order to end aggression and genocide but also caused collateral civilian harm. Some may claim that its bad intention in Variant 3 makes Weden's intervention morally impermissible. By contrast, I believe that, despite its bad intention, if ending aggression and genocide would come about and the harm to civilians caused by attacks necessary to stop genocide is proportionate to ending aggression and genocide, then if Weden knows it will end genocide and acts on condition that it will, its war can be morally permissible. Weden is doing the right act for a bad reason.

(I emphasize that Weden's starting war in these cases is permissible not on grounds that ending aggression and genocide are so important a "supreme emergency" that side constraints on wrong acts should be ignored. For example, it could still be impermissible for Weden to drop bombs on civilians so they become human tinder for setting afire German military operations, thus ending aggression and genocide.)

I have noted that my conclusion about Weden Oil Variant 3 conflicts with the part of the DDE that claims that intending evil will make an act impermissible. But it should be noted that my earlier conclusion may also conflict with the DDE. That is, the DDE, arguably, justifies proportional and unintended side-effect harm only if one's act is necessary to *pursuing* a greater good. That suggests that if a greater good will occur but is not intended, it cannot help justify lesser side-effect harms. By contrast, I argued that a factor that could be a just cause need not be intended in order to help justify starting a war that will have some bad effects.

Now suppose, in another hypothetical, that Sweden, not Weden, had stopping the aggression and genocide as its only goal in starting war against Germany. Suppose its only means of stopping these would be to attack the Germans so that they lose control over Norway's oil resources, for Germany will be unable to engage in aggression and genocide without money from oil. (Call this the Sweden Oil Case.) Attacking would not be ruled out because there would be some collateral civilian deaths or because Norway would then sell oil to Sweden for the first time. Notice also that if Sweden acted for the sake of a factor that can justify going to war (ending aggression and genocide), it might *condition* its action on some factor that does not justify going to war. For example, stopping aggression and genocide could be very expensive for the Swedes. This expense might defeat their acting on their good intentions, and they might permissibly refuse to pursue their just cause because of the expense. However, they could foresee that Norway once saved would grant them access to cheap oil that would offset their expenses to a degree that made war to stop genocide economically feasible. My claim so far is that the very different ultimate or instrumental intentions of Weden and Sweden would not make Weden's war impermissible, if Sweden's war would be permissible.

B. INTENTIONS, CONDITIONS, AND MEANS

So far, I have imagined that Weden conditioned its starting war on the expected effect of aggression and genocide ending. I have also imagined that Sweden conditioned its war on the expected effect of its getting oil. That is, Weden allows itself to seek oil resources only if aggression and genocide will also end, and Sweden allows itself to end aggression and genocide only if it will get oil resources. Weden may have the end-aggression-and-genocide condition on acting so that it will have a pretext for its intervention, and so not be chargeable by other countries on which it relies with an unjust attack on Norway. That it would not pursue resources (or killing civilians) unless the prospect of ending aggression and genocide were present to defeat the charge of an impermissible (even murderous) attack need not mean that it really has two intentions (goals) in acting, namely, to get resources and to stop the aggression and genocide. (In Weden Oil Case Variant 1, it does intend to end aggression and genocide, though only as a means to getting oil. However, in Variant 2, where ending aggression and genocide is a side effect that it does not need for oil, even this is not true.)

Consider a case that may help to clarify the distinction between acting in order to achieve an effect (whether as an ultimate goal or as a means to a further goal) and acting because an effect will occur but not in order that it occur.[6] In the Party Case, I wish to have a party for my friends and me to have fun but I will not have the party if I have to clean up the mess after it. (The prospect of the mess would be a defeater of my pursuing my goal.) I learn of psychological studies that show that if my friends have a good time at the party, they will have a feeling of indebtedness that will lead them to clean up. I give the party only because I know that my doing so will cause them to feel indebted *and* clean up the mess. I take advantage of the foreseen side effect of their feelings of indebtedness; I would not give a party if I did not think this side effect would happen. Giving the party on condition that they will feel indebted and clean up is consistent, I believe, with my not giving the party in order to (with the intention to) make my friends feel indebted. My goal in giving the party is for us to have fun. I do not give a party in order to produce an effect that will defeat a defeater of my act. Giving the party on condition that they will clean up is also consistent with my refusing to aim at making my friends feel indebted in any other way, and so it would not be a goal I have in giving the party or doing anything else that I produce feelings of indebtedness.[7]

Possibly one could describe me as having the following goal: "To have a party where there is no mess for me to clean up."[8] Suppose this is my goal. Then my friends' feeling indebted and cleaning up is something I must bring about by my actions if my goal is to be achieved. Some may say that this implies that making my friends feel indebted is a means to my goal.[9] Suppose this is true. Then it might be asked, as a rational agent must I not be committed to intending the means necessary to my goal? In fact, I believe that a rational agent need not intend a necessary means (understood as what he must bring about if his goal is to be achieved) to his goal; in particular, he can continue to intend his goal without intending such a means to it when he sees that these means (i.e., making his friends feel indebted) will be a side effect of something else he does, such as having the party.[10]

Similarly, one could possibly describe Weden as having the goal of "starting war to get oil (or kill civilians) with no international retaliation." That is, its starting war in pursuit of oil (or killing civilians) could be defeated by the prospect of retaliation by other countries. Some may say that when it acts only if it also has the pretext of ending aggression and genocide, its ending aggression and genocide is a means to its goal of avoiding retaliation.[11] Suppose Weden's doing something that brings about what is necessary to avoid retaliation amounts to its bringing about the means to its goal of avoiding retaliation. Then its stopping aggression and genocide would be a means to its goal of no retaliation. But that need not imply that Weden intends this means to its goal, as it can continue to intend its goal without intending these means to it when it foresees that these means—in the sense of what is necessary that it do if its goal is to be brought about—will be a side effect of something else it does.

In Sweden's case, it is possible to describe its goal as "stopping aggression and genocide at no great expense." It can pursue this goal without intending one of its means to it (on one understanding of means)—namely, getting oil—when it foresees that getting oil will be a side effect of its ending genocide.

Hence, the fact that Weden conditionalizes starting war on its stopping aggression and genocide need not mean that it acts with the intention to stop aggression and genocide, and the fact that Sweden conditionalizes its war on oil resources coming need not mean that it acts with the intention to get resources.

As described above, one way to understand the relation between a goal of action and the condition of action is that the latter can provide a nongoal reason to act because it defeats a potential defeater of an act undertaken for a reason that is a goal. (On this understanding, a condition of action is a sort of reason for action in a broad sense—a consideration in favor of action—though not the object of an intention.) So, in the Party Case, my goal is to have a fun party but my acting to have the party would be defeated by there being a mess to clean up. However, a side effect of my having the party, namely a feeling of indebtedness in my guests, will help defeat the defeater, as the guests will clean up the mess. In an imaginary case of Wedish intervention, Weden's aim of starting a war for oil would be defeated by the prospect of international retaliation except that the side effect of attacking to get oil, namely stopping aggression and genocide, defeats the defeater. In the imaginary case of Sweden's war, Sweden's aim of stopping aggression and genocide would be defeated by its shortage of money, except that the side effect of intervention—getting oil resources—defeats the defeater.

To further support this conclusion that acting on condition of an effect one will produce need not involve intending the effect, we can imagine that Weden would not be willing to do anything extra (however easy or otherwise unobjectionable) so that ending aggression and genocide *is* a side effect of its intervention, if ending these would not follow just as a consequence of what it must do to acquire oil. (Call this Weden Oil Case Variant 4.) Likewise, we can imagine that I would not be willing to do anything (however easy or otherwise unobjectionable) so that my friends' feeling indebted is a side effect of my giving a party. In particular, I could refuse to make it the case that giving the party made them feel indebted, if it did not already do so, consistent with *taking advantage of* the party's making them feel indebted so that I can give a party without a mess. And Weden could refuse to make it the case that getting oil causes aggression and genocide to end, consistent with taking advantage of the fact that what it does to get oil ends these so that it can get oil without retaliation. But it would be hard to reconcile refusing to do anything extra to make one's friends feel indebted, if a reasonable person already *intended* to bring about the feeling of indebtedness. Similarly, it would be hard to reconcile refusing to do anything extra to end aggression and genocide if Weden already intended to end these in order to avoid retaliation.

(It is easy to imagine that I would not do anything extra to make my friends feel indebted, since a feeling of indebtedness in others can be unpleasant for them. However, rescuing people from aggression and genocide is good for them, so it is harder to imagine why Weden would refuse to aim *at making it the case* that its act of seeking oil also leads to ending the two evils. After all, doing this would be good for Norwegians and also good for Weden, as it would allow it to get oil. We could imagine the following hypothetical that makes sense of such a refusal: Weden wants an effect to come about that could justify its starting war, so that it does not engage in behavior likely to anger some nations. However, it also does not want to alienate other nations in the world that are in favor of the aggression and genocide and who consider their ending to be bad. Such nations might object to Weden's doing anything extra with the aim of eliminating the evils, even as a mere means to its getting oil, and yet accept Weden's acting to get oil though ending aggression and genocide is a side effect of its getting oil.[12])

The results of my discussion of the hypothetical Wedish and Swedish cases are summarized in Table 3. The table shows that a factor or factors that could be a just cause for beginning a war (such as ending aggression and genocide) may be an agent's ultimate goal, merely his means to his goal, or a side effect of his act that he also takes as a condition of his action. If it is one of the latter two, the fact that the agent's goal could not be a just cause and is even a positive evil, need not, per se, rule out the permissibility of its going to war. Hence, if having a right reason for war involves having a right intention, whether ultimate or intermediary (as in intending the factor that could be a just cause only as a means to some other goal), then lacking a right intention need not, per se, rule out the permissibility of starting a war.[13] In addition, having a bad intention instead of a right intention, need not per se rule out the permissibility of starting a war. Of course, insofar as what one takes as a goal of action is

Table 3:

	Agent attitude		
	Goal	Side effect taken as condition	Mere means
Justifying cause	End aggression	End aggression	End power of group aggressing
Nonjustifying cause	Get oil	Get oil	End power of group controlling oil

of significance in predicting whether one will do other impermissible acts, the goal of one's act could be relevant to a consequentialist evaluation of the permissibility of beginning a war. It could also be relevant to a non consequentialist analysis insofar as this is in part concerned with consequences. This does not give it intrinsic deontological significance in relation to permissibility; it gives it consequentialist significance as a predictor of other impermissible acts.

C. INTENTION AND PERMISSIBILITY

The cases I have discussed led me to reject the requirement of a right intention in order to start war, but only on very limited grounds, namely that taking the presence of a factor that can be a just cause for starting war as a condition of action (even for non-moral reasons) can suffice. Then I extended the argument a bit by concluding that acting on condition could suffice even in the presence of a bad intention.

There are much more radical ways to reject right intention as necessary for permissibility. They would also rule out the necessity of taking a factor that could be a just cause as a condition of action. For example, suppose Weden would have started war to get oil, even if, counterfactually, this would not have also stopped aggression and genocide. However, circumstances are such that it knows that its act will stop aggression and genocide. I do not think we can say that Weden acted impermissibly just because it would have acted impermissibly in different circumstances.[14]

An even more radical approach would eliminate the knowledge condition. For suppose Weden did not know aggression and genocide would be eliminated by its intervention. Would the fact that its invasion did eliminate aggression and genocide still make its war permissible?[15] In this case, Weden was actually attempting to do something in the absence of factors that could justify its invasion, but it failed in its attempt.

The most straightforward defense of the more radical views claims that when an agent has a wrong intention, he does not do an act for the sake of the properties that make the act permissible or required—and he acts for a bad reason—but that need not make the act itself lose any of the properties that make it permissible or required. This is shown, Thomas Scanlon has argued, by the fact that in most (not all) cases an agent can decide whether an act is permissible or required by considering properties and effects the act would have independently of considering with what intention she would do the act.[16]

However, sometimes an act might lose properties that make it permissible or required due to an agent's intention. Consider that in the Weden cases that I have discussed, the good constituted by the just cause (ending genocide) would come to pass regardless of the intention of the agents who brought it about. In other cases this might not be so. Suppose a just cause were "stopping aggression to preserve national sovereignty valued by a nation's people" (rather than just "stopping aggression"), and a nation aggressed against would itself stop the aggression. Further, suppose its aim in starting a defensive war was only to acquire oil resources from its opponents. Though preserving sovereignty would be a side effect of doing this, the people of the nation do not value their national independence, per se, and would not fight even in part in order to preserve it per se. This nation's actual intentions (and lack of intention) implies that it cannot achieve the designated just cause because it will not stop aggression that preserves national sovereignty valued by a nation's people. In this case, I believe, the fact that an agent acts only for oil makes its act lack the property that could make it permissible.

Return to cases in which the just cause would come to pass regardless of the intention of the agents who bring it about. Here is another way to explain why intention does not matter to permissibility in these cases. We ordinarily think that the primary reason why an act that interferes with a nation's sovereignty or harms its citizens is wrong is that it has properties to which the people of that nation would be justified in objecting on their own behalf, in the sense that the properties would give them a right that the act not be done. I believe members of the nation(s) Weden enters or attacks could reasonably resent the inappropriate or bad intention of Weden because of the attitude to them it expresses. This is what Scanlon calls the meaning of the act. But this would not necessarily give them a right that Weden not so intend. Further, when even members of the entered or attacked nations should agree (because it is true) that elimination of aggression and genocide can justify war and is not ruled out by oil eventually going to Weden, I do not think they have a right that Weden not act unless it acts for the right reason (or at least for a reason that they do not justifiably resent). Of course, sometimes people have no right that others not act on bad intentions even when the act produces no important goods whose pursuit is either a duty or supererogatory, and even when the act is wrong. That is people often have a moral right to do wrong (e.g., read pornography). These cases differ from the ones we are examining in that Weden's act produces relevant goods and Weden conditions its acts on producing the goods. So the sense of "morally permissible" with which we are concerned is stronger than "have a right to do" despite bad intentions.

I have here confined myself to a less radical claim concerning when intention does not affect permissibility—that acting on condition of a factor that could be a just cause can suffice for permissibility—in order to retain some positive reference by an agent to factors that have positive moral significance, and so that the acts of Weden and Sweden will overlap in a wide range of counterfactual circumstances. The less radical claim also models a fairly typical type of agent: one who acts for the wrong reason but does not merely accidentally conform to externally correct behavior. As such, we are evaluating the permissibility of acts whose origins involve a fairly common psychological profile.

II. *Some Issues in Satisfying Proportionality*

One focus of Section I was whether a factor that could help justify starting a war if it were taken as a just cause *could* also help justify a war if it occurred as a side effect, at least when it is taken as a condition of going to war. Now our question is whether a factor that *could not* help to justify starting a war by being a just cause could help to *justify* starting a war in some other way. That is, can factors other than a certain few that are thought to be just causes of war play a role, for example, in satisfying the proportionality condition and thus, in determining whether starting a war is justified? (In Section I, we have seen that factors that could *not* be justifying aims in starting a war [such as getting oil] could play a role in an agent's deciding to go to war without making the act impermissible, but this is not the same as their playing a role in making his going to war justified or permissible.)

Here is an example of how the *ad bellum* proportionality condition in the morality of war is to be employed: Stopping aggression may justify starting a war only if the direct bad effects of a war[17] are proportional to relevant good effects that will result. Among the good effects that are relevant and could weigh against the bad effects are stopping the aggression which is a just cause for war. Proportionality is *not* a matter of whether the bad effects are proportional to harms that have been done to a victim on whose behalf a war is fought, but (at least in part) whether the bad effects are proportional to the harm the victim will avoid by war.[18] Suppose (for the sake of argument) that some good effects, such as economic benefits or deterrence of future aggression, could not be just causes for starting a war.[19] Could they permissibly weigh against relevant bad effects of war in a proportionality calculation for justifying war? If they can, then while they could *not* be just causes, they could help *determine* that starting war is permissible (in the sense of not unjust).

I shall discuss this question by examining views that Jeff McMahan and Thomas Hurka seem to have held (at least at one time), and try to develop an alternative account. I emphasize that I am here concerned with when we may start a war, not with when we may continue a war in progress rather than end it.[20]

A. THE NO SENSE ARGUMENT AND NARROW AND WIDE PROPORTIONALITY

Jeff McMahan at one time argued that factors that cannot be just causes cannot play a part in an *ad bellum* proportionality calculation, at least to outweigh death and maiming of persons in war. He said,[21]

The achievement of aims that are specified by a just cause can contribute to the satisfaction of the *ad bellum* proportionality requirement. No other goods that might be realized by war may weigh against the bad effects that would be attributable to the war in determining whether war would be proportionate....A just cause is necessarily connected with moral liability to attack on the part of those targeted for attack. The basis for liability is moral responsibility for a wrong that belligerent action would either prevent or somehow rectify....

To see that only the prevention or correction of wrongs[22] can weigh against the evils of war in the proportionality calculation, consider what would follow if other desirable goals were allowed to count as well. I am assuming that people can become morally *liable* to be killed or maimed only by virtue of action (which I take to include knowingly allowing things to happen) that wrongs or threatens to wrong others. If that is right and we assume that desirable goals unconnected with the prevention or correction of wrongs can count in the proportionality calculation, it follows that the achievement of these goals could justify (or contribute to the justification for) deliberately killing or maiming innocent (that is, nonliable) people....

For suppose there is a just cause for war against a certain country, and that going to war against that country could be expected also to mitigate the harshness of the religious oppression that many of its citizens suffer. It may seem that the expectation of alleviating religious oppression could contribute to the justification for war by weighing against the bad effects in the proportionality calculation, at least if those warred against were responsible for the oppression. But this seems to imply that *the pursuit of an end* that is insufficient to justify killing and maiming—namely, alleviating religious oppression—can contribute to the justification for an activity—war—that necessarily involves killing and maiming. And that makes no sense.[23]

Following Thomas Hurka, I shall call this McMahan's "No Sense Argument."

One issue in interpreting the No Sense Argument is whether McMahan was concerned only with those liable to be killed for a just cause (either deliberately or as a side effect) because of their actions also being killed (deliberately or as a side effect) for a nonjust cause (i.e., for doing things for which they are not liable to be killed)? Or was he also concerned with side-effect harm to those not liable to be killed for a just cause (e.g., to civilians who have done no wrong acts)? (Civilians are not usually thought to be liable to being killed, as McMahan uses the term "liable." For example, they are not usually thought to have done things that make them liable to deliberate killing or even side-effect killing. This need not imply that it is always impermissible to do what causes their deaths as side effects. However, unlike those liable to being killed, civilians can have their rights infringed if they will be killed or maimed even as side effects of military action, and compensation may be owed to them or to others on their behalf.[24])

Elsewhere, McMahan says that whether our response to wrongdoers is proportional to their wrong is a matter of "narrow proportionality." By contrast, he says that whether killing and maiming (and other bad effects to innocents)—both targeted and side effect—are proportional to goods to be achieved by war is a matter of "wide proportionality."[25]

It is worth pointing out that a wrongdoer may be liable to more harm than he threatens in order to stop his wrongdoing. So a narrowly pro-portionate response to stopping aggression could involve more harm to a wrongdoer than he threatens to do to a victim. Consider a domestic analogy. Suppose a wrongdoer threatens only to paralyze your legs. Killing him could be a proportional response, if this is necessary to stop him. If he only threatens to punch you, killing would not be proportion-ate, even if it were the only way of stopping the aggression.

It is also worth noting that a response to multiple wrongdoers can satisfy narrow proportionality so long as the response to each is proportional to his wrongdoing. This is very clear in a domestic case, for if each of many people is trying to paralyze you (or some other innocent person), it could be a proportionate response to kill all the wrongdoers to prevent the paral-ysis of one person. On the basis of this sort of case, one might describe the determination of a proportional response to wrongdoing as involving "pairwise comparison" (providing a new use for a procedure used in dis-tributive justice): One compares the wrong to be avoided with what would have to be done to each wrongdoer one at a time, and if there is no violation of proportionality in any individual comparison then there is no violation tout court. This is a nonaggregative approach to determining proportionality of response to wrongdoers. It contrasts with adding up and weighing in aggregate wrongdoers' lost lives against a single victim's paralysis. It also contrasts with a balancing approach which would involve the harm to a victim being weighed once against a proportionate response to one wrongdoer and in this way being given all the weight it is allowed to have, with the remaining wrongdoers' lives counting against self-defense.

However, applying the domestic analogy to war seems to imply that war cannot be disproportionate on account of the total number of aggressors harmed. (One might individuate aggressors by thinking of different nations or, alternatively, individual enemy soldiers.) I believe that both Hurka and McMahan accept the domestic analogy for narrow proportionality. Yet, both think the Falklands War was disproportionate to the aggression committed because of the number of soldiers killed, not because of a disproportionate response to any one soldier. Their position on the Falklands War suggests there are complications in applying the way of dealing with multiple aggressors in a domestic context to *jus ad bellum*. I shall not pursue this issue here.

I shall consider the No Sense Argument first on the assumption that McMahan was concerned with only those who are liable to be killed and maimed (mostly deliberately) for a just cause and subsequently consider the Argument under the assumption that he was also concerned with side-effect deaths to nonwrongdoing civilians. However, before proceeding, we should be aware of another part of McMahan's discussion. He goes on to say,

> Not all of the bad effects of war involve killing or maiming. There are many lesser types of bad effect. Even if the relief or mitigation of minor religious oppression can*not* justify killing or maiming, perhaps it can weigh against, and therefore justify, the infliction of some of the lesser bad effects of war. If that is so, perhaps certain expected good effects that do not rise to the level of just cause can count in the proportionality calculation, provided that they are weighed only against lesser expected harms and not against the inevitable killing and maiming.[26]

What McMahan says here might be accounted for by the following thought: If there were no just cause for war, we might still permissibly do what ends religious oppression even if this causes certain bad effects less than killing and maiming, either deliberately or as side effects. For example, ending religious oppression may justify deliberately doing something that destabilizes the oppressive regime despite bad economic effects on those not responsible for oppression. If this is so, then ending religious oppression can also play a role in outweighing bad economic effects when they are caused by destabilizing a regime in a war started for a just cause.

Similarly, what McMahan says in the second quote might be supplemented so that good economic effects on innocents in a war can weigh against bad *economic* effects on the same innocents in the war, and so help determine whether war is permissible. This is so, even though good economic effects cannot justify starting a war and the bad economic effects occur to those not responsible for creating a cause for war. For example, suppose war will ruin the economy of the country that has done wrong and that this side effect will be very hard on nonwrongdoing civilians. This might be a reason not to pursue a just cause. But suppose we know that after the war quickly ends, economic reconstruction by the winning side will almost immediately make everyone economically better off than they would otherwise have been. Then, the bad economic effects may no longer make war impermissible.[27]

B. DELIBERATE HARM

Now consider the No Sense Argument solely with respect to deliberate (targeted) killing and maiming of wrongdoers. McMahan's concern with pursuing aims other than the just cause by deliberately attacking wrongdoers is that they may not be liable to being killed in that way for those aims because (1) their wrongdoing does not involve undermining those aims and/or (2) pursuit of those aims is not a just cause for such killing even against those whose wrongdoing does involve undermining the aims. Hence, if pursuing the just cause itself would necessitate deliberate attacks on wrongdoers that are out of proportion to what wrongdoers are liable for purposes of achieving the just cause, those excessive attacks cannot be justified by the fact that another, nonjust-cause aim will also be achieved.

1. *Hurka's View*. Thomas Hurka has argued against McMahan's views on narrow proportionality. He believes that factors other than those that can be independent just causes may determine whether we start a war by helping to justify even deliberate killing and maiming.[28] Indeed, Hurka thinks that given the presence of an independent just cause we may permissibly have additional *aims*, none of which would justify starting a war on its own, that we seek in going to war. He thinks that deterrence of other potential wrongdoers, incapacitation of an offender (whose acts give rise to a just cause) from doing future harm, and correcting less serious human rights violations of the offender are not just causes but can be such additional aims. He calls them conditional just causes, as acting on them is conditional on having a standard, independent just cause such as stopping aggression. (He does not include economic aims among these conditional just causes.) He thinks that these aims can help offset bad effects of war that would otherwise stand in the way of pursuing the independent just cause. In this respect, his argument might only suggest offsetting side-effect killing and maiming (of innocent civilians and those liable to attack). However, he further thinks that allowing such additional aims to help determine when a war is not unjust is analogous to deciding that it is permissible to punish a criminal in a certain way because doing so would deter other potential criminals, even though it would be unjust to treat an innocent person in ways comparable to punishment merely in order to deter others. He also says that in order to deter others from crime, we could permissibly "punish somewhat more harshly" a criminal than we otherwise would.[29] It is this supposed analogy to punishment that suggests he is trying to justify additional deliberate killing of wrong-doers in war, not merely side-effect harms.

Hurka says that there are at least two different cases in which deterrence of other potential wrongdoers could permissibly be sought in going to war. In his view, in neither case would deterrence be a standard, independent just cause. In one case, due to an aggressor's act, the deterrence level of potential wrongdoers worldwide would be diminished from what it was previously (or would have been), if we do not respond to the aggression. Here we seek to restore deterrence to its level (or expected level) ex ante the wrongdoer's act. In the second case, Hurka describes our additional aim as increasing deterrence over the level it was prior to the wrongdoer's act (or over the level it would have been if not for the aggressor's act). McMahan would have special difficulty with this second case. He thinks that wrongdoers are liable to be targeted only because of the wrongs they do and in proportion to the significance of the wrongs. If a wrongdoer's aggressive behavior makes it morally responsible for reduction in deterrence, it may be liable to certain harms to bring back deterrence to the ex ante level. The wrongdoer is not, however, liable to such harm merely to *increase* deterrence when it either had no part in reducing deterrence or we would aim to increase deterrence *above* the level that did (or would have) existed without its wrong act. McMahan's additional view, implied by the No Sense Argument, is that if the harm to which a wrongdoer is liable in order to maintain deterrence did not *itself* justify deliberate killing and maiming, then the country's having reduced deterrence can play no part in justifying deliberate killing and maiming in a war against it. (I should note that McMahan, unlike Hurka, may in fact think that, at least sometimes, deterrence alone can be a just cause for action against a wrongdoer. Simply for the sake of argument, I shall assume they agree that deterrence alone is not such a just cause.)

2. *The Punishment Analogy.* Hurka argues that deliberate harm out of proportion to achieving the independent just cause itself could be proportional to achieving the just cause and the conditional aim together. On Hurka's view, what can be done to an aggressor—someone against whom one has a just cause—only for the sake of achieving an aim such as deterrence is not the same as what could be done to a nonwrongdoer for this aim. For example, he thinks that if a country has committed aggression, one may do things to it that one may not do to a nonaggressor for the sake of achieving deterrence (that even goes beyond correcting for reduction in deterrence due to the aggressor's wrongdoing). This "higher charge" (call it y) may then be added to the "charge" extractable just for aggressing (call it n). The total might amount to (and so justify) the deliberate killing actually required to successfully pursue the war just against aggression (e.g., $n + y$). Hence, the second aim can make the war satisfy a narrow proportionality requirement.

The defense of doing to an aggressor more for deterrence than one could do to nonaggressors is supposed to stem from the punishment analogy. He says of punishing an individual criminal that "we may treat someone somewhat more harshly" in order to achieve deterrence of others' criminal acts. (This is deliberate harsher treatment.) In the war case, "treat more harshly" would mean that it becomes permissible (including we would have a right) to cause deliberate damage to the higher degree $n + y$ for the two aims when it was *not permissible* to cause such harm to the aggressor nation for the aim of stopping aggression alone, and it was not permissible to cause y to a nonaggressor for the sake of deterrence. Hence, if the punishment case were truly analogous to the war case, it would involve punishment of excessive severity, which it would *not* be permissible to impose just in order to punish a criminal for some crime he had committed, *becoming permissible* because it will also deter other criminals' acts. That is, suppose punishment p is proportional to the crime committed but punishment $p + r$ is excessive, where r is less than p. It might be that $p + r$ *is* not excessive if adding r to a criminal's punishment p also deters others' crimes. This is so even though r alone would be excessive if done to a noncriminal to increase deterrence.

3. *Objections.* (a) However, I doubt that this is a correct account of how a punishment $(p + r)$ that was impermissible can become permissible. Rather, when we say in the context of punishment that "we may treat someone somewhat more harshly" in order to achieve deterrence, I think the "may" does not indicate a change in what it would be permissible for us to do (e.g., a change from p to $p + r$), in the sense of what we have a right to do. It may indicate a change in what it makes sense to do or what we will actually do. It might also involve a change in what we "should" do in the sense that there would be no good moral reason to do all that we have a right to do (rather than, for example, be merciful) if deterrence would not occur. Suppose, contrary to the previous assumption, that it were permissible (in the sense of "we have a right") to impose a punishment of severity $p + r$ on someone just in virtue of what he has done, independent of considerations of deterrence. This does not mean that we would have a duty to impose it; we might correctly impose less. Suppose we were actually going to impose less (only p). Then we find

out that imposing $p + r$ would deter others, and so we decide to do so. Here the possibility of deterrence does not change what it is strictly *permissible for us to do* to the criminal, only what it makes moral sense for us to actually do. We treat the person somewhat more harshly than we otherwise would have, but not more harshly than we otherwise had a right to treat him. Indeed, we may now have a *duty* to treat him more harshly than we previously would have but not because we have acquired a right to treat him more harshly.

So understood, it does indeed seem permissible to impose up to the limit of what a criminal's crime permits ($p + r$), but for the aim of deterrence. However, this interpretation of "treat someone somewhat more harshly" is not what is called for by Hurka's discussion of the role of deterrence as a conditional aim in starting a war. This is because that role involved *a change in what it is permissible* to do (i.e., go to war to stop aggression at necessary cost $n + y$ to the aggressor) on account of a second aim being achieved.[30]

(b) In any case, the most appropriate analogy to starting a war involving deliberate killing seems to be apprehension of a criminal to stop his crime rather than punishing a criminal. Consider a variety of cases involving targeted harm in apprehending a criminal:

(i) It is impermissible to stop a crime by killing the criminal, but it is permissible to do something slightly less bad to stop him. However, it is only physically possible to stop him by killing him.

(ii) It is permissible to stop a crime by killing the criminal if this is necessary. However, it is possible to stop the crime by shooting him in the leg instead.

(iii) It is permissible to stop a crime by killing the criminal, and doing so would be necessary to stop him. However, we decide not to do it.

Could we justify killing the criminal in any of these cases on the ground that, we may suppose, only in this way could we also deter other criminals from similar or worse crimes? I do not think that deterrence makes killing him permissible in either (i) or (ii).[31] In (iii), it might make killing the criminal, which we all along had a right to do, what we should do. However, only (i) seems to be analogous to the problem Hurka is dealing with in starting war.[32]

Another difference between (ii) and (iii) is also important. In (iii), the harm *required* (and permitted) to stop the criminal *itself* also brings deterrence. In (ii), harm required to stop the criminal (shooting him in the leg) does *not* itself bring about deterrence. Only the additional costs we would impose are imagined to provide deterrence. The question in (ii) is whether it is acceptable to make use of the upper limit on what we may permissibly do to the criminal if it were necessary to stop him, by combining a lesser harm that is actually necessary and sufficient to stop the criminal with the additional harm to him required to deter. Unlike what is true in the punishment case discussed earlier, I think it is not acceptable. This may be because in punishing we would impose what a criminal deserves (on a retributivist view) but in stopping crime we would impose harm to which a criminal would be liable to stop his act without this being what he deserves. This could also be true in the case of war, if aggressors are liable to up to cost n but we could stop them for less. Extracting cost n so that deterrence may also be achieved may not be permissible. (Cases in which more harm would be done for the sake of deterring others than is necessary and sufficient to stop the criminal will be important in later discussion.) The difference between (ii) and war cases we are considering is that the higher cost in (ii) would be permissible just to stop the criminal, if it were necessary, but not permissible to pursue only the just cause.

I conclude that Hurka's punishment analogy, at least, does not show that when a country is guilty of aggression, it becomes permissible to impose more deliberate killing on it, when this is needed to stop its aggression on the ground that we will also achieve a conditional aim. I also conclude that an analogy with domestic crime apprehension does not yield an argument against McMahan's No Sense Argument insofar as it deals with deliberate killing.[33] This leaves it open that the conclusion for which Hurka wishes to argue is correct and a better argument could be available.

4. *Helping the Aggressor*. However, there seem to be other cases where it would not be unjust to deliberately harm a wrongdoer for the sake of a good for which he is not liable to be harmed, contrary to the No Sense

Argument. Consider the following Help the Aggressor Case 1: Suppose that we cannot achieve the just cause of stopping an aggressor country unless we deliberately kill more of its soldiers than would be justified by achieving the just cause alone. If we do not achieve the just cause, deterrence will decline and another aggressor country will not be deterred from soon invading the current aggressor. The future aggressor will deliberately kill those of the current aggressor's soldiers that we need to kill to achieve the original just cause plus many more soldiers. Hence, it is no worse for some of the excess soldiers we would kill and better for others, if we do what will achieve deterrence. It seems to be morally permissible to harm the soldiers even if they are not liable to being killed by us in order to achieve the original just cause, given that this is also good for the current aggressor country and its soldiers. (This is true even if, for some reason, it could not be a permissible just cause for us to stop the future attacker. I discuss such cases below also.)

C. SIDE-EFFECT DEATHS

Now consider the No Sense Argument on the assumption that it is meant to encompass side-effect killings and maimings of nonliable civilians. (I shall consider only nonliable civilians in the enemy nation rather than a country's own civilians or neutral civilians.[34]) The concern would then be that if these harms are out of proportion to accomplishing the just cause alone, what Hurka calls conditional aims cannot help make the harms satisfy wide proportionality.

I have elsewhere argued that ordinarily, in nonwar contexts at least, not all bad side effects on innocents are created equal. Creating bad side effects as a result of deflecting threats (as in the famous Trolley Case) may be permissible when creating the same bad effects as a result of creating new threats is not permissible. In war it is bad effects of creating new threats that is usually at issue, so results from deflection cases should not be relied upon.[35]

In addition, bad effects that result from the achievement of a greater good (even when this creates a new threat) may be easier to justify than bad side effects of mere means to the greater good. For example, suppose that the only way to save five people from a car headed to them is to push them to the side of the road. Unfortunately, we know that their being there will move another person from that spot and over a cliff. Alternatively, the five being there will cause some rocks to tumble, killing a person below. I think it is permissible to move the five in these cases. I think this is because a greater good (of five saved) is what causes the bad side effect. But suppose that the only way to move the five from the road is to use a device that will crush a bystander. Here a mere means to a greater good causes the bad side effect. I think that using the device is impermissible.[36] If we were to apply principles of harm that incorporate such distinctions, it might be permissible to drop bombs on a military factory if side-effect deaths of civilians were caused by the destruction of the factory itself but not if they were caused by the bombs. This is not a distinction recognized in standard just war theory. Elsewhere, I have suggested that war may introduce factors that alter the general morality of harming in certain ways. (I shall return to this issue a bit at the end of this chapter.[37]) Hence, in this discussion, except where specifically noted, I shall not distinguish morally between bad side effects of means that achieve a just cause (and that achieve a military mission within war) and bad side effects of the achievement of a just cause (and of the achievement of a military mission within war).

1. *Goal and Condition.* One way to put the reasoning implicit in the No Sense Argument is as follows:

> If factor Q is not an aim that is a just cause for starting a war, it cannot be any sort of justifying reason to start a war.[38] But if Q plays a role in our decision to go to war by being a positive factor weighed against a negative factor in a proportionality calculation, then it will be a justifying reason to start a war. This is wrong.

One problem with this argument might be that it fails to distinguish the possible senses in which Q can be a reason that justifies action. One is the sense in which Q is a *goal* that we seek to accomplish. In this sense, we aim at the occurrence of Q. The second sense is one in which the occurrence of Q is a *condition* of action, as discussed in Section I. That is, we think that the act is justified in part because Q will occur, and we would not act if Q did not occur, but we do not act in order that Q occur. Hence, even if it is neither permissible for Q to be an *aim* for whose sake we are justified in starting a war (as in just cause), *nor* permissible for Q to be a conditional aim in Hurka's sense, it could still be a condition whose occurrence—for example, as a side effect of war—makes it permissible to start a war.

Notice that in the first quote given above (p. 132), McMahan first speaks of "goals unconnected with the prevention or correction of wrongs" (that give a just cause). "Goals" is the aim sense of reason for action. He then speaks of the "expectation of alleviating religious oppression...weighing against the bad effects" and says that if it does so weigh, it will involve "the pursuit of an end that is insufficient to justify killing and maiming" contributing to the justification for war (p. 132). But if one acts on condition of a certain good effect, this need not mean that one acts "in pursuit of an end" (as argued in Section I). That is, we must consider the possibility that even if an effect should not be taken as an aim in order to justify starting a war, or even as a conditional aim, it might permissibly help justify war when it is taken as a condition on starting a war for some other aim.[39]

However, in the second quote given above (p. 134), McMahan says that mitigation of religious oppression perhaps can "weigh against, and therefore, justify some lesser bad effects of war. If that is so...expected good effects can count in a proportionality calculation...." As he is here speaking of "expected good effects," it is open that these good effects do not serve as aims but merely as conditions on action and that without being aims, they can weigh against bad effects and help justify going to war.

Recall the Party Case presented in Section I to illustrate the distinction between aims and conditions, both of which can be justifying reasons in the broad sense of considerations in favor of an act. In the Party Case, I wish to have a party but will not have one if I have to clean up the mess after it. I learn of studies proving that if friends have a good time at the party, a feeling of indebtedness will lead them to clean up. I give the party only because I know doing so will cause them to feel indebted and clean up. This is consistent with my believing that it is wrong for me to aim at making my friends feel indebted and so it should not be even one of my aims in giving the party that I produce feelings of indebtedness. As noted above, one way to understand the relation between the aim of action and the condition of action is that the latter can provide a reason (in a nongoal sense) to act when it defeats a potential defeater of an act undertaken for a certain aim. So in the Party Case, my aim is to have a fun party but my act of having the party would be defeated by my having to clean up a mess. However, a side effect of my having the party, namely a feeling of indebtedness in my guests, will help defeat the defeater as the guests will clean up the mess.

Consider another case, involving *jus in bello* (i.e., justice in the waging of war), in which it might be held that we should not aim at something even though it is undeniably *good* (rather than [arguably] bad, like death or feelings of indebtedness in friends). A soldier is to bomb a factory for the justifiable aim of destroying munitions in it. However, a side effect of this factory blowing up is that the local food supply of a large community is much diminished. This side effect might defeat the justification for the action because the harm is out of proportion to the good that we aim at. However, another known side effect of the factory blowing up is that the people will move for work to another area where there is plentiful food. Their temporarily being in transit is a cost proportional to the military aim. Call this the Relocation Case. It may not be an appropriate aim, whether independent or conditional (in Hurka's sense), for soldiers on a military mission to act in order to relocate civilians to better living conditions.[40] Nevertheless, the relocation as a side effect outweighs damage to their food supply so as to make their overall loss proportional to the mission. The argument in this case depends on the idea that *an unintended* good (i.e., relocation to plentiful food), not only a good we intend, can outweigh bad side effects.[41] In this case, as in many proportionality calculations, we are weighing some bad that will occur (reduced local food supply for some people) against some good that will occur (increased food supply for the same people).[42]

But now consider a different *in bello* case that is like Relocation, except that in addition to causing the out-of-proportion damage to the food supply, the bombing will scare off local criminals from killing all the members of that same community. Call this the Scare the Criminals Case.[43] It may not be an appropriate aim, whether independent or conditional (in Hurka's sense), for soldiers who are on a wartime mission to also act *in order to* stop local criminals. Nevertheless, it might be argued, the side effect of preventing people from being killed outweighs damage to their food supply, and so it is a reason for the mission going forward. But the fact that the alternative to our bombing would be worse for these people than our bombing does not seem to make what actually happens to them—the loss in their food supply—proportional to the bombing of the munitions. Does this case, therefore, show that we need not satisfy the proportionality condition for our act to be permissible when the harm we cause to people is less than the harm others would have caused to the very same people?

The Scare the Criminals Case is unlike cases such as Relocation in which both good and bad effects actually occur. Rather, it involves a counterfactual bad state (death) being compared with a bad effect that will actually occur if bombing takes place (reduced food supply). When we consider what actually occurs if we bomb, we see only a very bad effect that itself (we are assuming) is out of proportion to the bombing. However, its occurrence actually represents an overall gain for those suffering it relative to their alternative state (dead). If we compare what actually occurs with what would have occurred, the bombing turns out to have no bad side effects and even a beneficial one. And this effect is certainly proportional to bombing the munitions. Hence, while Scare the Criminals involves a different way in which to determine proportionality than Relocation, it does not show that proportionality is not always a requirement.[44]

Here is a way to describe practical reasoning that is common to Relocation and Scare the Criminals: It would not be permissible for the soldiers to bomb the munitions plant if all this did was to profitably relocate people or stop criminals. By contrast, bombing the munitions plant in order to help win the war is permissible but only if the side-effect damage is not out of proportion to the good we achieve. The point is that in these cases (i) there are goods the soldiers do not act in order to achieve (and even should not act in order to achieve) (ii) whose occurrence as a side effect of what they do to win the war (iii) may imply that they *need not forgo bombing* for the sake of winning the war (iv) simply because destroying munitions would not alone justify the bad effects of bombing. The good side effects defeat a defeater of acting on an appropriate aim. (Call this Defeater Reasoning.)

The distinction between acting in order to bring about something and acting because something will occur is not, I believe, taken account of by the No Sense Argument. This is so, even though in the objection that McMahan himself raises to the argument (in the second quote), the good (relief from religious oppression) that outweighs a harm less than killing and maiming does not seem to be aimed at but merely expected. Hence, it is also possible that even if one cannot justify starting a war in order to deter other countries from aggressive acts, and even if one may not have such deterrence (contrary to Hurka) as a conditional aim, the fact that the war will have this effect could justifiably outweigh negative effects of going to war that would otherwise make pursuit of a just cause impermissible.

Furthermore, I shall now argue, this might be true even when the negative effects are deaths and maimings, which the No Sense Argument and the quoted addendum to it deny. Here is one such *ad bellum* case: Suppose that lives of innocent civilians that would be lost in war are out of proportion to the just cause of stopping an aggressor. However, if we do not fight, these civilians plus many others would soon be killed because other countries will not be deterred from soon attacking the country that is now an aggressor. In this case, the very civilians who would die from our attacks would have soon died in attacks anyway, along with other civilians, had the deterrent effect of our war not occurred. (Call this the Help the Aggressor Case 2.) Here, a deterrent effect that we should not start a war in order to produce and that might not even be an appropriate conditional aim may nevertheless be a reason why it is not unjust to fight the war, in the sense that we may act because (or on condition that) the effect occurs. And this is so, even though the number of those killed, considered on its own and not in conjunction with counterfactual harm that would have occured, remains out of proportion to the just cause.

We could also imagine the following variant on the Scare the Criminals Case that involves death and maiming *in bello*: The needed attack on the military facility will *kill* many civilians and this effect could rule out the attack. However, if we do not attack the facility and thereby scare off criminals, the criminals will kill these same people plus many others anyway, at the same time. That the people killed will be no worse off if we attack than if we do not might justify proceeding with our attack needed to achieve the just cause. This is a case in which *killings and maimings* (not just reduction in food supply) are the bad side effects that are justified in part by a good side effect (scaring the criminals).[45]

We might also construct an *ad bellum* case in which proportionality is satisfied despite killings that actually occur (rather than by counterfactuals). Suppose war for the just cause will cause side-effect killing and maiming to nonliable people that is disproportionate to the just cause alone. But it will also have the side effect of uncovering otherwise irretrievable national religious artifacts. Suppose it would have been reasonable for the people who die as the side effect of our military attacks to have been willing to run a high risk of death as a side effect of blasting undertaken to uncover those artifacts. (Call this the Artifacts Case.) Even though we should not start a war in order to uncover such artifacts and it is not even an appropriate conditional *aim* for us to uncover them, perhaps their being uncovered as a side effect could make the comparable wartime risk of killing civilians satisfy wide proportionality.

In this case, we can expect that people would reasonably have no objection to deaths caused when artifacts are uncovered. However, a stronger argument for the permissibility of causing side-effect deaths might be available if the good effect of bombing was something for which those killed had a duty to risk their lives.[46] Such a case might involve the wartime bombing removing a fatal threat to the children of those civilians who will die as the effect of the bombing. This is on the assumption that the parents would have a duty to allow procedures to save their children that cause the relevant risk of side-effect death to themselves. (Call this the Parents Case.) An even more credible case would involve a variant on Help the Aggressor 2 (or Scare the Criminals), in which our war causes side-effect civilian deaths that, in fact, would not otherwise have occurred but nevertheless decreases the ex ante chances of those same civilians of being killed (to 25 percent) from what it would otherwise have been (50 percent) due to other aggressors or criminals.

Most generally, suppose what is necessary to pursue a just cause would lead to more side-effect killings of civilians than is proportional to the just cause. Then it may be permissible to act if a good effect also occurs for which the civilians would reasonably, or should obligatorily, take the sort of risk of bad side effects that our bombing will cause. The good effect can (but need not) include the avoidance of a worse effect for them that would have occurred if we had not acted.[47]

Cases like Relocation, Scare the Criminals, and Help the Aggressor 2 may rebut the No Sense Argument but they have limited implications. This is because even though there is serious harm to innocent civilians (even killing and maiming), our harmful war can leave the very people harmed no worse, or even better, off than they would otherwise be and can also save other people who would have died. At worst, the outcome in terms of actual harms will be worse but ex ante expected harms will be the same or better for each of a certain set of people whether we act or not. Similarly, in the Party Case and the case where economic reconstruction rebuilds the economy, the "mess" that would be the bad effect of having the party or the war is completely undone by the other effect of the party or war, namely that the guests or the winning side "cleans up the mess" for the very people to whom the mess occurs. Here the outcome in terms of the ultimate state of no "mess" is the same or better whether or not we act.[48] In the Artifacts and Parents Cases, there is a good to those harmed that seems to compensate them for their being harmed.

Thus none of these war cases meets the following conditions: (i) a bad effect (such as deaths of civilians) continues to make the outcome worse *for one group of people* than it would have been if we had not acted; and yet (ii) the worsening in this respect is thought to be *morally outweighed* by (perhaps unintended) greater good effects to another group of people, benefits to whom are not a source of compensation to the first group; (iii) when achieving those greater good effects would not be a just cause for starting a war. Call cases that meet these conditions "morally outweighing" cases, and ones like Help the Aggressor "equivalent or compensated" cases.[49] I shall return to morally outweighing cases below.

In using the distinction between acting in order to produce an effect and acting only because one will produce an effect in discussing the No Sense Argument, I have referred to permissible and impermissible aims. But recall that in Section I, I argued that the factor whose presence could justify starting a war need not actually be the factor at which an agent aims in order for his starting the war to be permissible. For example, suppose that the facts are like those in Help the Aggressor but an agent's only aim in going to war against country A is to deter another nation from justly attacking A in the near future. This is because the agent fears that if the nation conquers A, its power will increase relative to its own. Such deterrence of a just attack could not justify starting a war against A. However, if an agent starts a war against A that stops A's current aggression against B, this will deter soon-to-occur just attack against A itself. The future attack would have produced more civilian deaths in A than would be produced by war now. Even if the number of side-effect deaths of war now would otherwise have defeated the just cause of stopping A's aggression against B, that fewer of the same people will die than would have from soon-to-occur attack on A could help justify starting the war. In this case, a factor (deterring a just attack) that is our agent's goal would only be a condition on action of an agent whose ultimate aim was the just cause (stopping A's aggression). However, because a factor that could be a just cause for starting war against A is present and is even a condition of our agent's act, it is permissible for *our* agent to start the war.

2. *Asymmetrical Justification for Harm.* Now let us consider further possible implications of the goal/condition distinction bearing on how to do *ad bellum* proportionality calculations.

(a) *Additive Approach to Costs.* First, note that if McMahan supported the No Sense Argument for side-effect killings, he could still accept that an additional aim had a role in determining proportionality if (i) stopping a country's aggression can justify both a deliberate attack on its wrongdoers (and also *some* side-effect harms to them) and (ii) seeking an additional aim (e.g., deterrence of future aggression) could justify causing the remaining side-effect killings. Suppose stopping a country's aggression can be justified if no more than n deaths occur to its wrongdoers and civilians. However, in actuality, stopping aggression must cause $n + x$ deaths, where x is less than n. Suppose seeking deterrence would be a permissible aim, if it had the side effect of killing only x people as a side effect, even in a nation that had *not* aggressed. ("x" is less than "y" that we said Hurka would permit to be deliberately imposed on a wrongdoer for deterrence.) This, in effect, means deterrence need not be an aim conditional on a just cause, if it is only necessary that seeking it cause x side-effect deaths. McMahan might then agree that achieving the just cause and deterrence would justify attacking an aggressor when this resulted in x side-effect deaths plus n targeted and side effect ones. This could be so, even though the x deaths resulted only from what is necessary and sufficient to stop the aggression itself, at least if stopping the aggression or the means necessary to this are necessary to produce deterrence.[50] Because harm that could permissibly be caused for deterrence on its own is added to harm that could permissibly be caused to stop aggression, this approach to justifying costs of war can be called additive. (McMahan may, in fact, deny that deterrence on its own could justify any side-effect deaths, but we could now imagine this was not true for the sake of argument.)

Hurka also uses an additive approach to costs. It is just that, unlike McMahan, he thinks that conditional on pursuing a just cause, we may do more to an aggressor for the sake of deterrence than we may do to nonwrongdoers, whether by targeting or side-effect harm. The additional amount that may be done ("y") gets added to n that is proportional to stopping aggression, so that $n + y$ actually necessary to stop aggression is proportional to the good produced.[51]

(b) *Objections.* I have concerns about this additive approach to costs. First, suppose that an agent would aim at deterrence as well as at ending aggression when harm caused by war would be out of proportion to ending aggression alone but not out of proportion to achieving both aims. Given an additive approach to costs, it would be odd for such an agent to be *unwilling* to start a war seeking both aims at this cost (e.g., $n + x$), even when conditions change and stopping aggression *alone could be done* with less harm that *is* proportionate to stopping aggression alone (i.e., n). After all, the agent was trying to achieve both aims within the higher cost permissible for both, and he can get this in either of two ways: (i) get deterrence as an effect of doing only what is necessary to stop aggression when stopping aggression requires causing harm $n + x$, or (ii) do what is necessary to stop aggression when this causes harm n, and in addition, do something extra to the aggressor that is necessary to get deterrence when this causes harm x. (This issue arises in a context where simply stopping aggression would not itself produce deterrence.)

It is true that the problem with which McMahan and Hurka deal *starts* when going to war to stop aggression (or for any other just cause) is expected to cause more killing and maiming than would be proportional to ending aggression alone. It is this additional harm caused by stopping aggression that Hurka suggests can be justified by conditional aims such as deterrence. However, my point is that the additive argument for this conclusion seems to have broader implications. For the argument claims that when a nation's aggression gives one a just cause for starting war that one will pursue, one may plan to pursue additional aims (such as deterrence) at a cost to the aggressor that is proportionate to that additional aim.[52] This argument does *not* specify that the costs that the additional aim is permitted to justify *must arise* from what is necessary to pursue (or what is a necessary effect of achieving) the independent just cause itself.

By contrast, an agent who sees achieving deterrence as only a *condition* of incurring the higher cost $n + x$ (or $n + y$) that results in (or from) stopping aggression could reasonably put avoiding cost x (or y) ahead of achieving deterrence, if it became possible to stop aggression at lower cost n. If the pattern of Defeater Reasoning described above applied, it could imply that we need not forgo achieving the just cause when achieving it requires $n + x$ killing and maiming, if deterrence will also come about. But the reasoning assumes (and requires) that the additional cost x (or y) that would be weighed against deterrence must be necessary to (or necessarily result from) achieving the just cause alone. Hence, if the just cause can be achieved without additional cost x or y, starting war to also achieve deterrence by doing what causes $x + n$ (or $x + y$) need not justify these greater costs. Nor would Defeater Reasoning justify us when starting war in employing separate means against the aggressor while we also pursue the just cause at cost n, just to achieve deterrence at cost x or y. We may have to plan to use the least harmful means necessary to achieve the just cause.

While Defeater Reasoning has these implications, it may not be alone in having them. That is, the difference between acting on condition of deterrence and acting in order to achieve deterrence is not *crucial* in order to rule out deciding to pursue deterrence at cost x when cost x is not necessary to help achieve the independent just cause. Rather, it is the role of the additional aim that is important, I believe. It is true that if deterrence is just a condition of action, and not an appropriate aim, an agent could reasonably refuse to do anything extra costing x just to achieve deterrence. This is because in doing something extra he would be aiming to produce deterrence rather than just taking advantage of the fact that deterrence will occur as a side effect of his going to war for the independent just cause. However, it is also sometimes possible for someone who would adopt deterrence as an additional *aim* not to be willing to do what causes cost x, if it becomes possible to achieve the independent just cause at the lower cost n.

To see this, suppose that stopping aggression must cost $n + x$, but deterrence is not an assured side effect of fighting the war at this higher cost. This might be because deterrence comes only when others know about the costs of war, and this knowledge would not automatically be available to other potential aggressors. Then in order not to forgo its aim of stopping aggression when this requires cost $n + x$, a nation might also permissibly adopt the *aim* of achieving deterrence by doing some morally innocent act, such as broadcasting news of the costs of war, in order to assure deterrence; it deliberately makes deterrence come about in order to help justify the unavoidable cost of stopping aggression.[53] Aiming to produce deterrence in this way would be consistent with the agent still having an obligation to pursue the just cause at the reduced cost n if this became possible. It is only *crucial* for starting the war that it be *costs necessary for achieving the just cause alone* that are to be justified and that the additional aim adopted does not involve extra costs not necessary to stop the aggression. The objection to the additive approach is to adding extra costs, *not* to adding extra aims per se.[54] Hence, focusing on defeater rather than goal-based reasons and focusing on goals that help cover costs necessary to achieve a just case are two different points.

The idea of "goods being proportional to harms" does not seem sufficient to capture this second point, because it does not distinguish between (a) seeking additional goods that will be proportional to some harms necessary to achieve an independent just cause and (b) seeking additional goods that will be proportional to additional harms that either are only necessary to achieve those goods themselves or are an unnecessarily harmful way to achieve the independent just cause. That is, the idea of goods proportional to harms does not capture the *asymmetry* between (i) adding goods to help justify costs necessary for achieving a standard just cause and (ii) *adding costs* so that more goods may be achieved. The former may be permissible when the latter is not, I suggest. I shall call this view the Asymmetrical Justification of Harm. It implies that it could be impermissible when starting a war to pursue deterrence at cost *x*, when one can also achieve the just cause at *n*, even if one could permissibly pursue deterrence at cost *x* on its own. Perhaps this is because once we plan to impose cost *n*, additional costs (our killing more people) should be avoided if they are not necessary for the just cause. (This last point shows that the essence of the Asymmetrical Justification of Harm is *not* that a particular cost *x* is proportional to an aim such as deterrence when this aim is necessary to allow us to achieve the just cause, but the cost is *not proportional* to this aim when it is not necessary to allow us to achieve the just cause.[55])

Hurka thinks that whether costs are proportional to achieving deterrence could vary depending on whether the costs fall on an aggressor or a nonaggressor, even when we are already imposing costs proportional to an independent just cause. My different suggestion here is that whether costs that are necessary and proportional to achieving deterrence are permissible might vary depending on whether they are necessary to achieve the independent just cause or instead to separately achieve deterrence (while we also achieve the just cause by lower costs). Asymmetrical Justification of Harm concerns the different ways in which the same states of affairs—composed of a certain harm (costs) and a certain good—may permissibly come about. One way (goods added for harms not due to the goods) might be permissible when the other way (harms added due to goods) is impermissible. This view has a form typical of nonconsequentialist views, that there can be a moral asymmetry between different ways of bringing about the same end-state. (For example, many have tried to defend the nonconsequentialist claim that an end-state in which someone dies can be permissibly brought about by letting someone die, even if it is impermissible to bring it about by killing someone, holding all other factors constant.[56])

Asymmetrical Justification of Harm seems especially important in cases involving (what I earlier referred to as) morally outweighing benefits as opposed to equivalent or compensating benefits. For example, suppose that achieving the just cause involved side-effect killing of an excessive number ($n + x$, *where x is considerably less than n*) of civilians in Group 1 of aggressor nation A. However, deterrence caused by achieving the just cause (or means to it) saved $2n$ *other* A civilians in (nonoverlapping) Group 2 who would otherwise soon have been killed due to another nation's attack on A. (Call this the Outweighing Help the Aggressor Case.) It is possible that we need not forgo doing what is necessary to achieve the just cause merely to avoid causing excessive ($n + x$) deaths to Group 1 when forgoing it would also mean *not* preventing $2n$ deaths to Group 2. (We are more likely to agree with this if we think of what we are doing to country A civilians as a whole, killing some but saving even more.[57]) Yet it is consistent with this implication that if we can, we must propose to achieve the just cause without harming $n + x$ of Group 1 civilians, even if this means not producing the deterrence that would save $2n$ of Group 2 civilians in A. Achieving the just cause without killing Group 1 civilians takes precedence over saving the lives of *other* A civilians (even from being killed by another aggressor or criminals). That is, the proposal is that we might not need to forgo achieving the just cause when good side effects of means *necessary* to achieve the just cause only outweigh bad effects but do not create "equivalent or better" effects. (Here not killing some in Group 1 does not take precedence over saving others in Group 2 in the sense that those saved can count toward achieving the just cause.) Yet it could be impermissible to weigh civilians we *save* from other attackers against other civilians we *kill* by means not necessary to achieve the just cause in plans for starting war.

Above, I suggested that McMahan's No Sense Argument does not distinguish between aims and conditions on action. Given what I have just said about the additive structure of an argument about costs, it seems that the Argument might also not distinguish between producing deterrence at cost x by (i) doing what is necessary to achieve a just cause and (ii) doing what is not necessary to achieve a just cause. Suppose both McMahan and Hurka believed that it would be wrong to start a war seeking both independent just cause and an additional aim at the original (higher) cost $n + x$ (or $n + y$) when the independent just cause could be achieved by n. Then, I suggest, it would be better for them to describe their position either as one in which deterrence is a condition (rather than a further aim) of achieving a standard just cause (e.g., ending aggression) at the higher cost $n + x$ (or $n + y$), or as one in which only the costs necessary to achieve the just cause are subject to being justified by the additional aim. In Hurka's case, these descriptions are preferable to one in which pursuing deterrence can be a conditional aim if one has (and pursues) an independent just cause for war.

Of course, if what was said in Section I is true, then the permissibility of an agent's act does not depend on whether a factor is actually his aim or a condition of his action, so long as factors that could justify starting a war *and* also make a war satisfy a properly formulated requirement on justifying harm are present. This is yet another reason why it will not matter whether deterrence is or is not an aim of particular agents. On the view that permissibility can be independent of intention, if deterrence could help justify a war were it a condition of action (as in Defeater Reasoning), then its presence could help make the war permissible even if it were the *primary* (let alone conditional) aim of a particular agent. (Of course, it could still make sense to say that this agent's aim is wrong and he should not have it, regardless of whether his having it makes his starting the war impermissible.)

3. *Morally Outweighing Cases in General.* At this point, it is worth reemphasizing that in considering arguments with both aims and conditions, we have dealt with morally outweighing and not only with equivalent or compensating cases. It might be said that the permissibility of harming in morally outweighing cases is a problem for both aim and condition types of arguments, because it allows saving some to outweigh killing others in cases where the causal structure would ordinarily not permit this. (That is, we are not dealing with redirection of threat cases, where killing to save seems to be permissible.[58]) In a sense, I agree that this is a problem. In this particular discussion, my only response is that standard just war theorists, as well as McMahan and Hurka, assume that it is sometimes permissible for a country to pursue goods that are said to only outweigh bad side effects that pursuing those goods cause.[59] For example, the effect of country M's stopping

country N's aggression may be that it saves its own, or another country's, civilians from victimization. But that good effect does not make N's harmed civilians no worse off than *they* would have been if M had not gone to war. Yet, for some reason, in the context of war, side-effect harm that our means will *cause* is thought to be outweighed by achieving the just cause. This is so, even though in nonwar contexts, we often reject comparable outweighing arguments. (I have already referred to this at the beginning of Section C.)

For example, suppose that we wish to perform lifesaving surgery on five people. However, a gas we must use will foreseeably have the bad side effect of killing an innocent bystander. (Call this the Gas Case.) It is thought to be impermissible to use means to aid the five people that cause the death of an innocent bystander, even though his death is a lesser harm relative to the good produced.[60] (In addition, suppose that the gas will have the good side effect of *saving* another innocent bystander. That this additional good would be a side effect rather than a greater good for which we act does not seem to make saving the five permissible when the effect is killing one. That is, we do not say that it is permissible to pursue some great good on condition that the lesser bad side effect is outweighed by a good side effect.) Yet McMahan, Hurka, and standard just war theorists accept that seeking to achieve just causes can justify using means that cause lesser side-effect harm to enemy civilians. These just causes only outweigh, they do not create merely equivalent or compensating effects.

Assume for argument's sake that we can permissibly outweigh side-effect killing and maiming of enemy civilians to degree n by pursuing a just cause. Then tradeoffs between good and bad side effects (such as between deterrence of aggression to Group 2 and killing and maiming of Group 1) might not be more problematic.[61]

III. *Conclusion*

In the first section of this chapter, I argued that from a nonconsequentialist point of view, sometimes one need not have a proper intention for it to be permissible to start a war. This is true, at least when one acts on condition of the presence of a factor that could be the object of a proper intention. I tried to distinguish between acting on condition of a factor and with the intention of bringing it about.

In the second section, I considered whether factors that could not provide a just cause for starting war could nevertheless help determine that we go to war, by helping to satisfy the proportionality condition. I supposed that a just cause (that could be a right reason) for war existed and asked whether certain additional goods that would be achieved could permissibly be balanced against harms that would otherwise be out of proportion to achieving the just cause. I examined some arguments for justifying excess deliberate fatalities by additional goods that would be produced. When the harms (including fatalities) are side effects, I argued that additional goods might help to justify a war by making it proportional. Even if we should not aim at these goods, we might act on condition that they occur. When additional goods make an outcome equivalent to or better than it would have been for the same people who are harmed, it will be morally easiest to use these goods to achieve proportionality. Outweighing harms to some by goods to others is more problematic. Furthermore, I argued, in deciding whether to start a war, there is a distinction between (i) the additional goods (whether conditions of action or aims) balancing out harms whose occurrence is necessary if the just cause is to be achieved and (ii) the additional goods balancing out harms not necessary if the just cause is to be achieved. The former (i) could be permissible, while the latter (ii) is not.

Notes

1. This chapter is dedicated to the memory of my uncle Vivian Oster, who passed away as a draft of it was being completed for presentation as an Uehiro Lecture, Oxford University, December 1, 2008. For comments, I am grateful to audience members at the Uehiro Lectures, the Boston University Philosophy Colloquium, the Copenhagen Conference on War, the Conference on War and Self-Defense, University of Sheffield, and the New York University Law School Colloquium on Law, Philosophy, and Social Theory. I am also indebted for comments on a written draft to Ronald

Dworkin, Shelly Kagan, Jeff McMahan, Thomas Nagel, Derek Parfit, Joseph Raz, Julian Savulescu, and Larry Temkin.

2. Throughout this chapter, I shall use "acting with the intention to," "acting in order to," and "acting for the sake of" interchangeably. There are cases, however, that show that the latter two categories are somewhat broader than the first (See Michael E. Bratman, *Intention, Plans, and Practical Reason* [Cambridge, MA: Harvard University Press, 1987]). I shall simply assume that if the first category involves a morally impermissible act, the latter two do as well. (Throughout, I am concerned only with moral permissibility.) It may be hard to understand how to apply the idea of intention to a collective agent such as a state. I shall not discuss this issue here but simply assume it is possible. For convenience, we can imagine that going to war depends on the decision of a chief executive of a legitimate government whose intentions can be isolated in the way individual's intentions are ordinarily.

3. All three of these components may not be necessary for permissibility. I am focusing on the minimal possible objection to the right reason requirement. In addition, in the absence of knowledge, its being reasonable to believe that a factor is or will be present, one's having this belief, and acting on condition of this reasonable belief, will also suffice.

4. I am thinking here not of Weden predicting its own future bad behavior, as its future behavior should, for the most part, be under its control. Rather, I am thinking of others, in a position to rule out Weden's acting, making predictions. (I owe this point to Johann Frick.)

5. Jeff McMahan expressed this view in his comments on an earlier version of this chapter.

6. I discussed the following case and argued for the distinction between acting in order (with the intention) to bring about an effect and acting on condition that (or because) one will bring about the effect in my *Intricate Ethics* (New York: Oxford University Press, 2007), among other places.

7. The distinction between acting on condition of producing an effect and acting in order to produce it also shows that the traditional Counterfactual Test for determining the presence of an intention is insufficient. That is, that one will act only if an effect will occur and will not act if, counterfactually, it would not, need not show that one intends the effect.

8. Ingmar Persson suggests this in his review of *Intricate Ethics* in "When We Have to Kill Vic," *Times Literary Supplement*, February 22, 2008.

9. Others may say that something I must do to achieve my goal is not a means to my goal unless it is done under the idea of reaching the goal (i.e., done for the sake of the goal). I owe this point to Ralph Wedgwood.

10. Under the alternative view of means described in the previous note, my point can just be put as: A rational agent who retains his goal need not intend to do what he knows it is necessary that he do if his goal is to be achieved.

11. This was suggested by Larry Temkin.

12. These other nations think there is a moral distinction between intentionally causing a bad effect and causing a merely foreseen bad effect, and they take ending genocide and aggression to be a bad effect. Weden need not think these nations are right in thinking these things in order to seek not to alienate them.

13. Some of these conclusions are also reached by David Enoch in his "Intending, Foreseeing, and the State," *Legal Theory* 13(2) (2007): 69–100. Enoch cites my discussion of the distinction between acting in order to achieve an effect and acting on condition (or because) one will cause an effect in his arguments. However, one of his concerns is to argue that when a country acts on condition that some *good* effect will occur, this should count to its moral credit, even if it is not one of its goals to bring about the good effect. I do not necessarily think this is correct. It will certainly depend on why it conditions its action on the good effect. If it cares that the good effect comes about because this will stop its being punished, this will not reflect well on it. If it cares that the good effect comes about just because it is good, this will reflect well on it. However, one must be careful to construct such a case so that bringing about the good does not just become a second goal of action. For then one would not have a case where the good is only a condition of action but rather a case in which two goals are jointly sufficient and necessary for action. For more on this, see *Intricate Ethics*, ch. 4.

14. I think Thomas Scanlon's views in *Moral Dimensions* (Cambridge, MA: Harvard University Press, 2008) imply this.

15. I think Judith Thomson's views as presented, for example, in *The Realm of Rights* (Cambridge, MA: Harvard University Press, 1992), imply this.

16. See his *Moral Dimensions*.

17. By "direct," I here mean to distinguish effects caused by acts of war from opportunities lost by going to war.

18. Thomas Hurka emphasizes this in his "Proportionality and the Morality of War," *Philosophy & Public Affairs* 33 (2005): 34–66; as does Jeff McMahan in his *Killing in War* (New York: Oxford University Press, 2009).

19. In "Making War (and Its Continuation) Unjust" (*European Journal of Philosophy* 9(3) [2001]: 328–43), I suggested that factors like deterrence that are not standard just causes for starting war could become so. For example, suppose one has a standard just cause (e.g., defeating aggression) but is unable to successfully defeat the current aggression. One could, however, successfully attack the current aggressor in a way that will deter others from future aggression against oneself. Starting this war could be permissible, I think, even if it were not permissible to resist an aggressor at the cost of innocent lives when this achieved no good at all. The permissibility of such a war could depend on whether the costs to innocents are proportional to achieving deterrence. Not all of what it might be permissible to do to defeat aggression may be permissible just to achieve deterrence. See also n. 55.

20. I have discussed the latter issue and what might justify continuing a war in my "Making War (and Its Continuation) Unjust."

21. "Just Cause in War," *Ethics & International Affairs* 19(3) (2005), p. 18. He now says he rejects this position.

22. McMahan is here referring to wrongs that can be just causes.

23. McMahan need not deny that religious oppression is a wrong, just not one whose correction can be a just cause for war. Note that there may be a distinction between factors that can justify continuing a war once started and factors that can justify starting a war. I assume McMahan is limiting his discussion to starting a war and, as noted above, that is what I shall discuss here.

24. McMahan himself raises challenges to the view that civilians are not liable (in his sense) to be killed in his *Killing in War*. Though he concludes that civilians usually do not do things that make them *liable* to being deliberately killed, he thinks they may be *liable* to side-effect harm. If this were true, it would mean that an attack could have proportionate civilian side-effect harms for which no compensating goods besides the just cause are needed. One would need compensating goods only for side-effect harms for which the civilians were not liable.

25. See his *Killing in War*. He actually treats combatants on the just side in a war as innocent victims, like civilians. I shall ignore this contentious issue here.

26. This role for nonjust-cause good effects may conflict with the position he took in an earlier article written with Robert McKim, "The Just War and the Gulf War," *Canadian Journal of Philosophy* 23(4) (Dec. 1993): 501–41. There they say: "Imagine that it was predictable that, because of the complicated effects of changes in the flow and pricing of oil that the Gulf War would have caused, the war would have had beneficial effects on the world

economy. If *P* (factors in a proportionality calculation) is unrestricted, these effects would weigh against the war's bad effects. This, however, is not only intuitively implausible, but is also incompatible with Just Cause. For economic benefits should not be part of the justification either for going to war or for any belligerent action during the war. Because of this, they cannot count in favor of war in the calculations required by *P*."

27. Having said that I plan to deal with both deliberate harm to wrongdoers and side-effect harm to civilians, I should note that subsequent to my writing the initial version of this chapter, McMahan has said (in *Killing in War*) that the No Sense Argument was intended to deal only with additional deliberate attacks on those already liable to be attacked for a just cause. And in comments on an earlier version of this chapter, McMahan says, "In the passage you quote [referring to first quote], I was thinking entirely in terms of the liability justification and thus was concerned only with what I call narrow proportionality—that is, whether a harm inflicted on someone does or does not exceed the degree of harm to which he is potentially liable. [Note that McMahan thinks wrongdoers could be liable to both targeted and side-effect killing and maiming.] The thought was that both in peacetime and in war, people who are responsible for lesser wrongs, such as religious oppression (wrongs that are not sufficient to make the perpetrators liable to be killed or maimed in order to prevent or rectify them) may be liable to suffer certain lesser harms either *as a means or as a side effect* of preventing or rectifying those lesser wrongs. Thus if going to war can be independently justified, it can be permissible in the course of war to inflict further, lesser harm on those who are liable to be killed or maimed because of the just cause, if those lesser harms are *necessary* and proportionate for the mitigation of religious oppression *for which those harmed are responsible*." This comment focuses on the difference between killing and maiming and other harms. It also speaks only of lesser harms to which one is liable. So it alone does not imply that McMahan would accept the extension to bad economic effects on civilians who are not liable to such bad effects. But perhaps McMahan should also be concerned with permissible harms to people who are not liable to such harms. I shall consider this issue below.

28. In defending this position in his "Liability and Just Cause" (*Ethics & International Affairs*, 21[2] [2007]: 199–218), Hurka claims that he is defending a position that McMahan previously defended in "The Just War and the Gulf War."

29. Ibid., "Liability and Just Cause."

30. However, Derek Parfit has pointed out (in comments on an earlier version of this chapter) that some believe that *only* wrongdoers may be punished *only* when this would do some good (e.g., deterrence). So wrongdoing is a necessary but not sufficient condition for any punishment. Suppose Hurka had meant by "we may treat someone somewhat more harshly" that we may punish a wrongdoer whom we would not otherwise have a right to punish at all when this will deter. Then the prospect of achieving deterrence would make punishment permissible that would not otherwise have been permissible. However, I do not think Hurka meant to adopt the position that any punishment would be impermissible unless it did deter, but a more retributivist view.

31. This is true in (i), even if the means *necessary* to stop his criminal activity would be what causes the deterrence.

32. Notice also that in the crime case, we are thinking of costs being imposed solely on the criminal, not civilian bystanders. It might be even harder to justify using a method to catch the criminal that imposes additional costs on *civilian* bystanders just because fighting the criminal will deter others' crime. Yet the latter can be at issue in the case of war. Indeed, suppose that stopping a crime would cause harm to people not actually involved in the criminal activity but who are members of a fraternal organization that the criminal represents. Would it be permissible to use methods to stop the criminal that kill his fellow members as a side effect, if we then deter criminals (from outside the organization) in the future? I do not think so. Pursuing a good end—even stopping criminal activity—in nonwar contexts seems to justify less harm to bystanders than many think pursuing a just cause in war can justify (a point we shall discuss further below).

33. Nor would this change, if we killed the criminal only on condition, not with the aim, that deterrence occur. I shall consider a possible role for the distinction between condition and aim in considering wide proportionality below.

34. I discuss possible moral differences among these civilians in "Failures of Just War Theory: Terror, Harm, and Justice," *Ethics* 114(4): 650–92.

35. This is a point that McMahan seems to ignore in *Killing in War*, p.289.

36. See, for example, my *Intricate Ethics*, ch. 5 for discussion of these claims. I considered what such distinctions among side effects would imply for conduct in war in my "Justifications for Killing Noncombatants in War," *Midwest Studies in Philosophy* 24 (2000): 219–28.

37. I discussed these issues in more detail in "Justifications for Killing Noncombatants in War," and in "Failures of Just War Theory."

38. At this point, I shall ignore McMahan's emendation concerning balancing good and bad effects less than killing and maiming (e.g., economic effects).

39. In his comments on the previous paragraph in an earlier version of this chapter, McMahan says he now accepts this point. He says, "I now agree with this entirely." He also says, "I do accept that nonjust cause good side effects can weigh against harms caused to innocent people, particularly if the harms to innocent people are also side effects. This agrees with your main point: that nonjust cause good effects can have a role in justification, though not as aims to be pursued....I now agree with your basic criticism—namely, I accept that even if nonjust cause goods can't have a justifying role as goals or ends, they have a justifying role in canceling out at least some corresponding side-effect harms, and in some cases, that justifying role can be a *condition* of permissibility, as you suggest." However, below, I shall argue that good effects that could not be independent just causes could also be goals and still have a role in justifying going to war. (Avishai Margalit has suggested [in his Tanner Lectures published as *On Compromise and Rotten Compromises* (Princeton: Princeton University Press, 2010)] that a group might be justified in waging a war for a standard just cause, such as stopping aggression, even though it could avoid the aggression by giving up something else to which it has a right [such as peaceful protest]. That is, it may go to war rather than give up it's right, even though it could be wrong to wage war to protect that right itself. This is a different way in which a factor that could not be a just cause for war can determine that a war occurs. I shall not discuss this sort of case in what follows, but I do discuss it in a revised version of "Making War [and Its Continuation] Unjust.")

40. Should they not be permitted to intend the relocation if it is merely a means to their being allowed to carry out the bombing? The point is that we can imagine a case in which even this would not be morally permitted (because, for example, aiming at something good for these civilians will offend a crucial ally), and yet bombing can proceed because they will relocate.

41. I emphasize this last point because, as noted above, the DDE (arguably) requires that some greater good be intended if it is to outweigh bad side effects. However, if permissibly intended goods cannot outweigh the bad side effect, my claim is that unintended goods can help do this. For more on the role of unintended goods, see *Intricate Ethics*, ch. 4, and "Terrorism and Intending Evil," Chapter 2 this volume.

42. As such, some may argue that it raises the issue of whether it is permissible to cause harm to a person merely to produce a good to him (see Seana Shiffrin's "Wrongful Life, Procreative Responsibility, and the Significance of Harm," *Legal Theory* 5 [1999]: 17–48). However, we are here considering whether it is permissible to pursue an important just cause when we produce good and bad side effects to the same people. This may be different from causing harm to someone when only a good for him would occur. In addition, in Relocation the harm is on the same dimension as the benefit (less food followed by more food). Shiffrin, I believe, focuses on cases where the harm is on a different dimension (broken leg) from the benefit (gold). The good we produce in the case that follows (in text), Scare the Criminals, is the avoidance of a worse harm and Shiffrin argues that it can be permissible to cause harm in order to diminish harm (by contrast with creating other sorts of goods).

43. This case is like the Massacre Case I first discussed in *Morality, Mortality, Vol.* 2 (New York: Oxford University Press, 1996).

44. I am grateful to Victor Tadros for discussion on this point.

45. Here is a domestic analogy: We can save five lives only by using a device that causes the side-effect deaths of two people who would soon otherwise be killed by criminals who are scared off by noise from our device. I believe it is permissible to use the device. McMahan has pointed out to me that the Scare the Criminals Cases also serve as counterexamples to part of Hurka's view. For Hurka holds that goods that are neither an independent just cause nor a conditional just cause and that arise from the means to the just cause, rather than from the achievement of the just cause itself, should not count in a wide proportionality calculation—that is, they do not weigh against harms to the innocent. The case he gives to illustrate this point involves collaboration between Arab nations and the United States in waging a war in Kuwait. It may be a side effect of the trust built up in such cooperation (the means to the just cause) that a solution to the Arab–Israeli problem will arise. Yet, Hurka says, this good effect should not count toward justifying the war. But in Scare the Criminals Cases, it seems permissible to count good effects of the means (noise from a device) in a wide-proportionality calculation. Hurka's discussion of McMahan, of course, is concerned with starting war (*jus ad bellum*) and the Scare the Criminals Cases are about acts *in* war (*jus in bello*). The Help the Aggressor Case 2 (in text) *is* about *jus ad bellum*, but in it the good effect of deterrence arises from our achieving the just cause, not just from a means to it. However, the follow-

ing third variant of Scare the Criminals that deals with starting war can show that good effects stemming from mere means may count in a wide proportionality calculation: Waging war, for the just cause of stopping aggression, could kill many civilians and be ruled out on this account. However, if we do not start the war, ordinary criminals would kill those same civilians *and* many others anyway. Fighting the war (the means to the just cause) will keep the criminals at bay. Even though stopping deaths from criminal activity in the aggressor country is neither an independent nor a conditional just cause, it seems this side effect of our means to a just cause could help justify starting the war. This is because only a subset of the very people who would die from criminal activity will be killed as side effects in the war. (The distinction Hurka is emphasizing is like one I drew between a *bad* [not good] effect arising from the means to a greater good [which could be impermissible] and its arising from the greater good itself [which could be permissible]. Hurka has criticized my use of this distinction in discussing war in his "Proportionality in the Morality of War," *Philosophy & Public Affairs* 33 [2005]: 34–66.)

46. I owe this point to Victor Tadros.

47. In the case of just war, I have been assuming that n deaths are proportional and the additional side-effect deaths that will occur are less than n. In this case, the just cause is important enough to merit more deaths (and even deliberate ones) than would be produced as additional side effects on civilians. But there could be war cases in which additional side-effect deaths are greater than n. There could also be domestic cases in which some party is liable to only a minor physical injury (e.g., a broken nose), but means necessary to stop his aggression cause side-effect deaths to those not liable to be killed. In the latter types of war and nonwar cases, does the general conclusion described in text still apply? Surprisingly, I think it may well apply. For example, suppose the only way to stop your nose from being broken is to do what breaks your attacker's nose and also has the side effect of killing a bystander. Suppose also that what you do that causes his death nevertheless decreased his chances of dying (to 50 percent) from what they would otherwise have been (100 percent). (For example, it scares murderers away from him.) Then it seems you need not refrain from defending yourself against the broken nose even though this causes a bystander's death and imposes costs on the person who is attacking you greater than he would have to pay just to reduce the bystander's chance of dying.

48. This is not to ignore the fact that creating a "mess" to be cleaned up can be a bad intermediate state to go through. I am assuming that the intermediate state is a bad effect proportional to the good of the party or the achievement of the just cause.

49. I am grateful to Derek Parfit for suggestions about appropriate titles for these types of cases.

50. This contrasts with a case in which $n + x$ is necessary to stop aggression, but deterrence could be achieved at far less cost unconnected with stopping aggression.

51. I am assuming that McMahan would forbid producing deterrence by imposing more side-effect harm on an aggressor than could be imposed on a nonaggressor for the same purpose. If this is wrong and he, like Hurka, would allow y rather than just x additional harm for deterrence, this would not affect my discussion of the additive structure.

52. On Hurka's view, the cost goes up from x to y in the special context of the nation being an aggressor.

53. Earlier, in discussing Relocation, Scare the Criminals, and Help the Aggressor, I emphasized that one could take advantage of a good side effect, even if it were not permissible to aim at the side effect even as a means to being able to pursue the just cause. And there may well be such cases. But there may also be cases where it is permissible to pursue an effect such as deterrence *as a means* to pursuing the just cause. It is these cases I am now discussing. So, for example, there might be a version of the Parents Case in which bombs do not automatically save children and it is permissible to arrange for them to do so, as a means of making the bombing permissible despite collateral harm to parents.

54. Adding costs might, however, become permissible once a war is being fought. On this, see my "Making War (and Its Continuation) Unjust." What if costs necessary to achieve a just cause are less than the maximum permitted (n)? May we impose up to n, if this will produce deterrence (as Ronald Dworkin suggested)? As the aggressor is only liable to cost n to achieve a just cause, and this does not necessarily imply that it is deserving of suffering cost n, we may have to restrict ourselves to achieving the just cause at less than n. This is based on what was said earlier (p.140) about capture of domestic criminals. However, Thomas Nagel suggests that domestically a court system can be relied on to produce deterrence, and this is not so in an international context. This could be relevant.

55. Furthermore, suppose we did not pursue a just cause because we would be unable to achieve it at acceptable costs. If it were possible, might it be per-

missible to at least achieve deterrence even by imposing the higher cost y on an aggressor (when cost n will *not* occur), given that cost y would have been a permissible cost at which to achieve the just cause? That is, though we have so far discussed cases where we also act on an independent just cause, perhaps it would be permissible to act on additional aims at higher than usual costs when we *have* a just cause but cannot act on it. Defeater Reasoning does *not* imply this conclusion, but there may well be justification for at least getting deterrence out of an aggressor whose aggression we cannot stop. The higher cost y may be justified as a transfer of some of the cost imposed on us by undefeated aggression. This is a case that supports Hurka's view that we may impose higher costs on aggressors than on non-aggressors to achieve deterrence. However, it is a special case that allows for an explanation different from the one he offers.

56. See *Morality, Mortality, Vol.* 2 for my attempt to do this. I am grateful to Shelly Kagan and Larry Temkin for pointing out this nonconsequentialist aspect of Asymmetrical Justification of Harm.

57. Hence, we might think differently about pursuing a just cause that involves killing $n + x$ of A's civilians when we then also save $2n$ of country C's civilians from attack.

58. I have discussed these cases, including the Trolley and Lazy Susan Cases, in my *Intricate Ethics*.

59. Allowing side-effect harm to be outweighed by achieving a just cause does not mean that these theories allow deliberate killing of civilians to be outweighed by achieving a just cause. In Chapter 2 on terrorism, we discussed deliberate killing of civilians.

60. This is Philippa Foot's case, discussed in her "The Problem of Abortion and the Doctrine of Double Effect," *Oxford Review* 5 (1967): 5–15. It forms part of her criticism of the Doctrine, which allows merely foreseen harms of means necessary to a greater good to be outweighed by greater good. McMahan has suggested that some may think that the Gas Case differs from war because it involves saving people from illness rather than from wrongdoing. But we could imagine that the five to be saved will be victims of an injustice, yet this will not make it permissible to use the gas, I think. A yet closer domestic analogy to war may involve using a gas against street criminals who will kill five people when the gas will kill a bystander as a side effect (and also save another bystander as a side effect). I do not think this would be permissible either.

61. Elsewhere, I have tried to explain to some degree the distinction between war and nonwar contexts. I suggested that the responsibility of innocent

civilians of an aggressor country to bear costs so that their country is not unjust, even though they have not acted incorrectly in bringing about aggression, might explain the permissibility of causing them some side-effect harm. See my "Failures of Just War Theory." However, it is not clear that Group 1 civilians have a comparable responsibility to Group 2 civilians (or to their country A) to contribute to reducing A civilian deaths overall by shouldering greater costs than are explained by their responsibilities to bear costs so that their country not be unjust. So outweighing between civilians of an aggressor nation and a victim nation may be easier to explain (or at least call on a different explanation) than outweighing between civilians within a nation.

BIBLIOGRAPHY

Bratman, Michael. *Intention, Plans, and Practical Reason*. (Cambridge, MA: Harvard University Press, 1987.)

Deen, Thalif. Millennium Summit. "UN Member States Struggle to Define Terrorism." July 25, 2005. www.globalpolicy.org/empire/terrorwar/un/2005/0725define.htm.

Enoch, David. "Intending, Foreseeing, and the State." *Legal Theory* 13(2) (2007): 69–100.

Foot, Philippa. "The Problem of Abortion and the Doctrine of Double Effect." *Oxford Review* 5 (1967): 5–15.

Herman, Barbara. "Murder and Mayhem." *The Practice of Moral Judgment*. (Cambridge, MA: Harvard University Press, 1996.)

Hurka, Thomas. "Proportionality in the Morality of War." *Philosophy & Public Affairs* 33 (2005): 34–66.

Hurka, Thomas. "Liability and Just Cause." *Ethics & International Affairs* 21(2) (2007): 199–218.

Kamm, F. M. "The Insanity Defense, Innocent Threats, and Limited Alternatives." *Criminal Justice Ethics* 6 (1987): 61–7.

Kamm, F. M. *Creation and Abortion*. (New York: Oxford University Press, 1992.)

Kamm, F. M. *Morality, Mortality, Vol. 1*. (New York: Oxford University Press, 1993.)

Kamm, F. M. *Morality, Mortality, Vol. 2*. (New York: Oxford University Press, 1996.)

Kamm, F. M. "Justifications for Killing Noncombatants in War." *Midwest Studies in Philosophy* 24 (2000): 219–28.

Kamm, F. M. "Making War (and Its Continuation) Unjust." *European Journal of Philosophy* 9(3) (2001): 328–43.

Kamm, F. M. "Failures of Just War Theory." *Ethics* 114 (July 2004): 650–92.

Kamm, F. M. *Intricate Ethics: Rights, Responsibilities, and Permissible Harm*. (New York: Oxford University Press, 2007.)

Kamm, F. M. "Terrorism and Several Moral Distinctions." *Legal Theory* 12 (Spring 2006): 19–69.

Kamm, F. M. "Terrorism and Intending Evil." *Philosophy & Public Affairs* 36 (2008): 157–86.

Kamm, F. M. "Types of Terror Bombing and Shifting Responsibility." In *Action, Ethics, and Responsibility*, eds. J. K. Campbell, M. O'Rourke, and H. Silverstein. (Cambridge, MA: MIT Press, 2010.)

Kamm, F. M. "Some Moral Issues about Killing in War." In *Oxford Handbook on Death*. (New York: Oxford University Press, forthcoming.)

Lang, Gerald. "Review of *Ethics and Humanity: Themes from the Philosophy of Jonathan Glover*." *Philosophical Reviews* (online), Aug. 11, 2010.

Margalit, Avishai. *On Compromise and Rotten Compromises*. (Princeton: Princeton University Press 2010.)

McMahan, Jeff. "Just Cause for War." *Ethics & International Affairs* 19(3) (2005): 1–21.

McMahan, Jeff. "Torture in Principle and in Practice." *Public Affairs Quarterly* 22 (April 2008): 91–108.

McMahan, Jeff. *Killing in War*. (Oxford: Clarendon Press, 2009.)

McMahan, Jeff and Robert McKim. "The Just War and the Gulf War." *Canadian Journal of Philosophy* 23(4) (Dec. 1993): 501–41.

Nagel, Thomas. "War and Massacre." *Philosophy & Public Affairs* 1 (Winter 1972): 123–44.

Nagel, Thomas. "Death." In *Mortal Questions*. (New York: Cambridge University Press, 1996.)

Persson, Ingmar. "When We Have to Kill Vic." *Times Literary Supplement*, Feb. 22, 2008.

Quinn, Warren. "Action, Intentions, and Consequences: The Doctrine of Double Effect." In *Morality and Action*. (New York: Cambridge University Press, 1993.)

Rawls, John. "Fifty Years after Hiroshima." *Dissent* (Summer 1995): 323–7.

Rodin, David. "Torture, Rights, and Values: Why the Prohibition of Torture is Absolute." New York: Carnegie Council, July 8, 2008. Available online at www.carnegiecouncil.org/resources/video/data/000068.

Scanlon, Thomas. "Preference and Urgency." *Journal of Philosophy* 72 (1975): 659–60.

Scanlon, Thomas. "Intention and Permissibility." *Proceedings of the Aristotelian Society, Suppl. Vol.* 74 (2000): 301–17.

Scanlon, Thomas. *Moral Dimension: Permissibility, Meaning, Blame*. (Cambridge, MA: Harvard University Press, 2008.)

Scheffler, Samuel. "Is Terrorism Morally Distinctive?" *The Journal of Political Philosophy* 14 (March 2006): 1–17.

Shiffrin, Seana. "Wrongful Life, Procreative Responsibility, and the Significance of Harm." *Legal Theory* 5 (1999): 17–48.

Shue, Henry. "Torture." *Philosophy & Public Affairs* 7 (Winter 1978): 124–43.

Sussman, David. "What's Wrong with Torture?" *Philosophy & Public Affairs* 33 (Winter 2004): 1-33. Available online at www3.interscience.wiley.com.

Thomson, Judith Jarvis. *The Realm of Rights.* (Cambridge, MA: Harvard University Press, 1990.)

Thomson, Judith Jarvis. "Self-Defense." *Philosophy & Public Affairs* 20 (1991): 283–310.

Waldron, Jeremy. "Terrorism and the Uses of Terror." *Journal of Ethics* 8 (2004): 5–35.

INDEX